THIS IS ME

THIS IS
me

LOVING THE PERSON YOU ARE TODAY

CHRISSY METZ

WITH KEVIN CARR O'LEARY

DEY ST.

An Imprint of WILLIAM MORROW

DEY ST.

I have changed the names of some individuals to protect their privacy.

THIS IS ME. Copyright © 2018 by 350 Degrees, Inc. All rights reserved. Printed in the United States of America. No part of this book may be used or reproduced in any manner whatsoever without written permission except in the case of brief quotations embodied in critical articles and reviews. For information, address HarperCollins Publishers, 195 Broadway, New York, NY 10007.

HarperCollins books may be purchased for educational, business, or sales promotional use. For information, please email the Special Markets Department at SPsales @harpercollins.com.

A hardcover edition of this book was published in 2018 by Dey Street, an imprint of William Morrow Publishers.

FIRST DEY STREET PAPERBACK EDITION PUBLISHED 2019.

Bee image by Victoria Belova/Shutterstock, Inc.

Library of Congress Cataloging-in-Publication Data has been applied for.

ISBN 978-0-06-283790-5

19 20 21 22 23 LSC 10 9 8 7 6 5 4 3 2 1

To: My mom, my Grams (Nama) and my sisters,
Monica, Morgana, and Abigail.

Some days she has no idea how she'll do it.
But every single day, it still gets done.

To the moon and back.
Chrissy XO

contents

INTRODUCTION

Hey, you.

Yes, *you*, lookin' all cute and stuff. Y'all don't even know how excited I am to finally talk with you. I have to tell you the weirdest thing: as I have been putting together this book for you, I have been seeing a lot of bees. Honeybees are meaningful to me because technically they're not supposed to be able to fly. We know they do, but in the 1930s French scientists "proved" they couldn't. Their reasoning was that it was aerodynamically impossible because honeybees' wings are too small to support the weight of their bodies. And yet, through some miracle, there they go, zipping through the air and soaring their little honeybee hearts out.

I get that. I'm not supposed to be able to fly either. As a kid, I was always too much. Or not enough. I heard it time and again, whether it came from my stepfather, who tormented me, or the first boy I loved, who would kiss me but never claim me. In Hollywood, I spent ten years hearing some form of "Yeah, not you" as I continued to look outward for validation and confidence. Meanwhile, I married and divorced a wonderful man because I didn't know how to love myself. It was only once I stopped looking for outside validation, and looked inward instead, that I realized I have all I need to fly.

Our true happiness is inside of us. Like me, everything you need to fly—to soar—has been inside you all along. Just as you are, you're enough.

I know we're going to talk about important things in this book, but I don't want it to be homework. I would rather we be somewhere chatting than taking a quiz. Still, much as in *This Is Us*, there might be a good cry involved every now and again. What I've learned from the show is that there are so many ways we can connect if we are willing to be vulnerable. Sharing the things that we're afraid will make us appear less in others' eyes makes us stronger. Because confidence is really trust in yourself, right? It has nothing to do with what someone else thinks of you; it's what you think of you. And as we collectively share our truths, I believe we are placing deposits into our own confidence bank. Not only does sharing your truth help other people, but then you feel good and come to realize your value. When you then build on that value and continue to be a positive person, you can be a light for others in getting out of *their* own way.

Lately I've been getting this question a lot in interviews: "If you could go back in time and tell yourself anything, what would it be?"

"Just try," is what I always say. For me, it was "I'm not gonna try to lose weight because if I can't lose a hundred pounds overnight, I ain't doin' it." Maybe for you, it's "I could never be a lawyer because I could never make it through law school." Or maybe you don't even want to think about what your dream would be because nothing has worked out for you before.

I consider myself a work in progress, and this book is full of the things I learned from the teachers, guides, and mentors I have encountered on my journey. It's my way of paying it forward from my perspective. This book isn't about getting taller, skinnier, richer, or more successful. It's about loving yourself and realizing the singular gifts we all have to offer each other. For me, I always had a love of storytelling. I wanted people to relate to *me*, so I started asking, "How do I relate to them?" Acting just happened to be the way I could connect to people. It took way more than a minute for me to achieve my dream, but I am glad I stayed around. Because there was some time when I didn't want to. I couldn't even get an audition most of the time. I got discouraged, but something told me to keep going. I showed up for myself. And it turned out to be acting.

I should tell you that a few years back, an American study revealed that those French scientists missed something special about the honeybee. They had assumed the bees flew like other insects. Pssht! They've got their own way. Bees beat their wings in a shorter arc than the conventional fly, but they do it faster. And when they need to lift a heavy load—in their case nectar, just as in our case a dream—they can beat their wings in a longer arc to get there.

And so, throughout this book, I have added Bee Mindful lessons from my life that I hope will help you as you carry your load. Let's get there together.

Love,
Chrissy

one

USE THE PRETTY NAPKIN

My cell rang just as I was leaving LAX and pulling onto the 405. Am I a Hollywood cliché, or what? A pleasant voice filled the car, saying a name I couldn't quite make out, followed by, "I'm Oprah Winfrey's chief of staff."

Now, I have a lot of funny friends, but Oprah? She's off-limits. She is not joke material, okay? But I played the caller's game, because the number-one rule of improv is Never Deny.

"Well, hi, Oprah's chief of staff," I said, sweetly and efficiently. "How are you?"

She repeated her name without missing a beat, probably used to people not believing her. "Ms. Winfrey asked me to reach out to check your availability for lunch at her home."

"Oh, okay, that's great," I said, playing along. This could be good.

I keep a calendar these days, which is so dang helpful but almost too grown-up for my liking. Point being, even if you figure it might be a joke, triple-check you don't double-book yourself the first time Oprah invites you to her house.

"Great," she said. "We'll be in touch."

Now, I'm sure a call from Oprah's camp should always be kept private, but there was one person I just had to tell. I mean, c'mon!

"Hey, Mom!" I said. "Guess who wants to maybe have lunch with me?"

The next call came while I was actually on the phone with my mom, and again I was coming home from the airport

"Hold on, Mom," I said, switching lines.

"Hi, Chrissy, it's Oprah."

Lawd-a-mercy.

Here's the thing, y'all. You think you'd be able to handle an out-of-the-blue call from Oprah, but I'm here to tell you, you're not. You start thinking about everything you've learned from her. All of her performances, her generosity, her wisdom, her Oprah-isms! She has been one of your mentors your whole life. And now, she's on the phone. WITH ME. Me! Just chatting with Ophs like we've been friends forever. I'm sure this is how everyone who speaks to Oprah feels. Of course, she immediately puts you at ease, even as you are trying to maintain your composure. The conversation happened so quickly, but here's what I distinctly remember: She loves *This Is Us* and knows I exist. Oh, and she wanted me to come to her house for lunch.

What would you wear to see Oprah? See? It's tough, right? Not too dressy, but something that says you've given your outfit thought. I went with an aubergine cotton dress from Torrid paired with a gray knit sweater, and navy-blue tie-up flats from Saks. It's about an hour's drive from my apartment in LA to her estate in Montecito, a beautiful area right on the south coast of Santa Barbara. My friends all thought I was crazy to drive myself. I value alone time and appreciate independence, okay? As I got closer to Montecito, I started second-guessing myself. I hadn't even gotten my car washed. Tryna catch me riding dirty, to Oprah's. (And she did.)

I pulled up to a very unassuming gate, and just as I thought I must have the wrong place, a young guy walked up. He was about twenty-one, with ginger hair, wearing a crisp polo.

"Can I help you?" he asked.

"Hi, yeah, I'm Chrissy Metz," I said. "I'm here to see Oprah. Oprah Winfrey. Ms. Winfrey."

"Oh, yeah, of course," he said, starting to walk up the driveway. "I'll lead you there."

"Um, well, do you want a ride?" I asked. "I can take you. I have a car."

He paused, very calm but trying not to laugh. "Uh, no thank you. I have the golf cart. You can follow me."

Oh God, I thought to myself. *"I have a car."* I was just trying to be helpful. You can't see the estate from the gate, and I didn't want the youngun' walking a 5K while I followed him.

We rounded the corner to this beautiful cobblestone driveway that went on forever. "Where are you taking me, Ginger Man?" I said out loud. Because it took about another half mile before I even saw anything that looked like a house. Finally, we rolled up to this huge fountain in the middle of a lake, and the gorgeous estate perfectly placed behind it.

I literally stopped my car when I saw the house.

"Oh my God." I was just about to grab my phone to take a picture when I checked myself. "Chrissy, are you trying to get kicked out before you're even in?" I asked myself in my full Gainesville voice. "No ma'am. No ma'am. You just put your little phone down right now."

Instead, I pulled into a small parking area, got out, and took in the scene. I was admiring the rolling hills when I turned to see a sweet-faced gentleman.

"Good afternoon, Miss Metz," he said, leading me to the main house.

"Hi, I'm here to see Oprah." Like, who else would I be there to see?

"Yes, Ms. Winfrey is expecting you." Then he handed me a beautiful crystal glass enveloped in a handwoven silk napkin. It was a ginger-and-mint iced tea, the most delicious tea this Southern girl ever did taste. I was nervous or parched, or both, so I of course started gulping it. To be fair, I am this way with all cold beverages. He left, and I was alone in this enormous foyer. I tried to play it cool and just take in everything around me. The beautiful grand piano, French doors that allow you to see out to the ocean . . . And then I heard it.

The voice.

"ChhRRRRRiissy!"

She said my name just like you'd want her to. Like she is introducing you to the world and your new life as someone she *likes*. She was wearing this cute navy-blue dress, with a cute ponytail, cute glasses, and cute sandals. Did I mention she is cute? Oprah is *cute*.

"Oh my gosh, thank you for having me," I said in one spill of words, overwhelmed by excitement and intense Oprah adoration. "Your house is so beautiful."

She took the smallest beat, and proceeded to give me one of the biggest lessons of my life.

"It is, isn't it?"

She said it calmly and without apology. She'd worked her butt off to live in a home she loves. She earned it and she deserves it, and she would do a disservice to herself and the beauty she surrounds herself with if she shrugged it off and deflected the compliment.

I'd been in Oprah's presence, what, two seconds? And already I had a life lesson—that it's okay for you to say, "I worked hard for what I have. I earned it and I am going to enjoy it, proudly." It only affirmed what I was learning: There is something that happens when you are grateful. You continue to receive blessings.

"Let's go to the garden room," she said.

Oprah led me into a room full of topiaries and even more French doors, where there was a round table set for lunch for two. Prior to my arrival I had been thoughtfully asked about food allergies and preferences. Thank you, Lord! I don't do the seafood, y'all. We sat down close to each other, and started with a spring-mix salad with apple, goat cheese, pecans, and a nice light dressing.

"These greens were just harvested today," she said.

"Oh wow," I said, thinking, *This is Oprah's garden salad.*

As we spoke, I did everything I could to keep eye contact without seeming like a crazy person. I mean, Oprah looked great. She was just back from New Zealand, where she was shooting *A Wrinkle in Time*. She told me about the blue of Lake Hawea, and her enthusiasm and love for the island affirmed my desire to visit the country one day.

She asked me questions about *This Is Us*, and about my life. She wanted to know how I got to where I was. As I opened up about my journey, she shared stories about her own trials in dealing with success, the early days when she started to really earn money and people came out of the woodwork with hands out.

"A stranger comes up and says, 'I changed your diaper when you was five years old,'" she said, with the Oprah folksy flourish. "And you're supposed to pay for their car. Or their big dream."

The next dish was placed on the table, this one a pesto pasta with truffle flakes. I told her how I had eighty-one cents in my bank account when I started *This Is Us*. And that now, I could visit my family in Florida whenever I wanted. The issue is that when you are not used to having money, your normal is scarcity. You start looking for ways to share your good fortune because you feel so guilty.

Oprah did that pursed-lip thing she does when she conveys that she heard you but doesn't necessarily agree with what you said. I told her that I had a really hard time trying to decide what I was going to buy everybody for Christmas, for instance. "I kept wondering, do I get something everybody can share?" I said. "Or, do I cap it off at a certain amount? Maybe get everyone something that they love, no matter what the price is. Not that I'm at that place financially yet . . ."

"Chrissy," she said, stopping me from sputtering. "Years ago, I spoke to my attorney because I was having such a hard time. I sat everyone down and I said, 'This is what you get, this is what you get.'"

"So, people stopped messing with you?"

"No, my family still asks me for money," she said. "But you have to decide what is right for *you*. What do you want to give? What do you want to buy them? It's not about how much it is. Because if you bought them a car, what are you going to buy them next year?"

Okay, there was Oprah Life Lesson #2, and I was only a few bites into my pasta. *You* have to be the one to decide what it is you want to give. It isn't always about money. It's your energy, it's your time, and it's your love. Those of us who are fortunate have to set boundaries, because others will imagine what you can give them and hold you accountable for that. Until their imagined need becomes a debt you owe them.

She then asked, as only Oprah can, about my relationship with my body. There had once been an ad for the *Oprah* show that went, "Emotional eaters, I am talking to YoooOOOooouuu." I remember how quickly and deeply that resonated with me. She talked to me then in my childhood home, and here I was talking to her in *her* home.

"I am working through a lot," I said. "There is so much

of my life that I just blocked out because it was too painful or too confusing. I realize now that it is all still there, still so close to the surface. I stuffed my feelings for so long, they have to come up and come out for there to be a real healing."

She nodded, and this time I knew she understood.

"Mentally and emotionally, I'm further on the journey," I said. "But I feel like my body doesn't reflect that yet. But it's coming. I know that."

I started to get a little teary-eyed. You should know this: I am a crier. I wasn't as a kid, but I am making up for it now. A raspberry-and-rosewater sorbet was served, and I hoped it would serve as a distraction while I pulled myself together. But there was Oprah watching as I raised my eyes to the ceiling and waved at my face to stop Mascara Falls.

"Girl," Oprah said, "use your napkin."

I looked down at this fine, silk white napkin with delicate handwoven edges.

"It's too nice," I said.

"Use the napkin."

I did as I was told. She smiled as I grimaced at the smudges of black.

"Good," she said.

I finally laughed and her smile got bigger. "You know," she said, "you're one of our lifetime's heroes."

I am not ashamed to say that I looked behind me to see who she was talking about.

"What?" I mean, was I living in an alternative universe? What the heck was in that ginger tea? She leaned in, so I did too.

"We all have a purpose," she said. "Some people are the tall oak trees, and some people are the beautiful bushes. But everyone has a purpose. There is nobody here on earth who doesn't have a path or a purpose. An innate destiny. Every human being who comes, comes called."

Yes, Oprah really talks like this.

Those words went right to my soul. Before I knew it, the dishes were cleared and Oprah rose from her seat.

"I'll walk you out," she said. Just as we were about to reach the front door, I looked around. "Oprah, what's your favorite room in your house?"

"Hmm," she said, thinking for a minute. "Probably my office or my bedroom. Come here. I'll show you."

"What?"

We walked up the stairs and she showed me her beautiful office. She told me she chose the color scheme based on the leaves of an olive tree, from the vibrant green of the top of the leaf to the bottom's pale white. Even the books in her library were covered to match. So beautiful.

"This is the Oprah Oval Office," I said.

Next, she led me to her bedroom, which was a nice big size but not crazy enormous. We stopped for a moment and looked out to see the rolling hills meet the road and eventually the shore. This really was the Promised Land.

Around the corner was the closet. I'd always dreamed of having a closet with an island in the middle—or having clothes to fill up a closet like that.

"Where are your shoes?" I pictured this wing of heels and flats, but she just pointed to a nice array of beautiful footwear neatly placed on shelves.

"There are some friends of mine who have a million pairs of shoes, but I don't," she said. "I wear every single one of these." C'mon, practicality.

We went back downstairs, and right before she walked me to the car, she said, "I want to show you my favorite spot."

Y'all! Oprah's favorite spot! She brought me to a little clearing by some trees where she meditates. "Next time," she said, walking me arm-in-arm, "bring a guest and your walking shoes. We'll walk around the grounds."

Next time?!

She walked me all the way to my car, and made no secret of giving it a bit of the side-eye.

"It's dirty," I said. "I'm sorry. This is embarrassing. I wouldn't presume you'd walk me to my car."

"I just wanted to see what you were working with," she said with a laugh.

What did it all mean?

As we hugged goodbye, I thanked her for inviting me

into her home, and she said I was exactly what she thought I'd be. I hopped in my car to head back to the valley. Three thoughts came to my mind:

1. How could all this have felt so normal?
2. I really need to wash my car.
3. I had dreamed that lunch into reality.

That last one is important. About ten years before, I took a day trip to Santa Barbara with my boyfriend, who later became my husband, who even later become my ex-husband. (We'll get to Marty later. Spoiler alert: He is a great guy and we are still friends. No, seriously.)

Marty and I had lunch at Giovanni's, a little pizzeria on Coast Village Road. I knew Oprah's famous Montecito estate was very close, and as I sat at that table, I thought, *I'm going to meet Oprah one day and live next door to her.* So, I said just that, out loud, in a joking way. "I want to be in Montecito someday, hanging out with Oprah." My wish came true because I put it out there. I truly believe that the things you want can happen, but it starts with asking.

Because honestly, I am someone who is still incredibly flattered that anyone knows my name, let alone Oprah. People ask me what the most surprising thing is about my life recently, and of course that lunch flashes in front of me. But it's all of it.

As a teenager, I was the girl sitting on the couch in Gainesville, watching Oprah because I didn't have a real mentor. In Los Angeles, I would watch *The Hollywood Reporter* actress roundtables with my friends because we couldn't afford acting lessons. I know firsthand that it's never too late for you and it doesn't matter what you look like. The universe responds when you really pursue your heart's desire.

THINK ABOUT WHAT YOU WANT.

I'll wait.

No, seriously. I am not leaving you alone on this page without you taking a moment to put a request out there. It can be hard to say what we really want. A lot of us, myself included, did not grow up with positive reinforcement. We were not told we could be or do anything we wanted, even if our wish was just to be happy. Whatever you've brought with you to this book, you can't allow those experiences, even traumas, to define you or limit you.

And maybe you are afraid that if you say what you want, someone will hear you. You fear the judgment of a loved one, or worry that your growth might be a threat to that person. My advice is to give people the opportunity to surprise you, and to grow *with* you as you become the person you want to be.

But right now, let's just talk amongst ourselves. You and me.

I will go first. Yesterday I was doing an interview with a gentleman from a magazine. It was a casual thing, and my hairdresser was hanging out with us in the room, for touch-ups. The interviewer suggested that since I sing on the show, maybe I should think about doing an album. My heart wants that. But I instinctively deflected.

"I don't know," I said. "You might be the only one who would buy it."

The words just hung there. He looked awkward, and I remembered that it doesn't make people feel good when you don't acknowledge the blessings you've been given. We are so afraid of believing that we deserve great things, especially if we do the hard work.

"You know what, wait," I said. "Yes, I will. I will record an album. I really, really want to. Thank you for thinking I can do that."

My hairdresser took me aside afterward. "Chrissy, it was so great that you corrected yourself in that moment. When you are confident in your abilities, it lets other people feel confident in theirs too. Sometimes we have to teach each other." I know I am still unlearning everything I was taught as a kid. When I was down, people told me that was where I would stay. But when you are *so* far down, the only way to go is up.

So, think about what you really want your life to be.

Picture yourself sitting proud and powerful, and imagine what a day in your life will look like. You might have to start with the protection of stating this as a joke, just as I had done in that pizzeria fantasizing about meeting Oprah. As you grow, I promise you that your joke will begin to look like a possibility. Once it's a possibility, you can and will make it a reality.

Say it out loud, and ask for it. When we meet, I want to hear all about it.

two

BOTTLE ROCKET
IN A BEER BOTTLE

Early last summer I visited my mom in Gainesville, Florida, where I'm from. We were sitting on the couch, going through a box of family pictures together. I found an old one of my father and me. We are on a swing set, and I am sitting on Mark's lap. That is what I call him, not Dad. Mark.

In the picture, I look about three years old and we are both smiling. It's the weirdest thing, because he looks happy to be with me. Proud, even. I stared at the photo for a second, trying to jog an actual memory of Mark being caring toward me.

"I don't remember having any kind of bonding experience with Mark," I told my mom.

She paused. "That's because you didn't."

"Oh daaaaaang, Mom," I said, laughing. She has absolutely no filter.

My mother divorced my father when I was eight, but she didn't say this to be malicious. She was just stating facts. It was a running joke that Mark only wanted boys for a baseball team.

Instead, his first child was my big sister, Monica. Two years later, things were looking up when Phillip arrived. And then five years later, here comes another girl. Me. It was well known that he was disappointed in the lineup.

Mark was in the navy, and our family moved to Yokosuka Naval Base in Japan six months after I was born. We would have gone sooner, but they had to wait for me to be old enough for vaccines. My earliest memories of my parents are of the cocktail parties they hosted for my father's navy buddies. I would try to stay up late with Monica and Phillip to not miss out on the fun of singalongs to the Doobie Brothers and Motown. My father was charming and a great storyteller. He seemed so happy.

My parents always had a lot of friends. My dad worked at a bar off base, and anyone who met my mom loved that she was a straight shooter. She was always looking for ways to make extra money, even becoming a taxi driver. I asked her later how she learned Japanese well enough to drive people around.

"I just did," she said.

That's my mom for you. She does what she has to do.

She is an incredible baker, and in Japan she developed a client base of service members who wanted a taste of home and locals who loved an exotic American chocolate cake. She was always working or baking, not to mention raising three kids with a guy who had no interest in diapers or housework. She could sew anything, and in Japan it was hard for her to find cute clothes that would fit me. I was a chubby little girl. There's a photo of me in this one dress she sewed with a giant elastic band that she made to look like a belt. I look at it now and I am like, "Girl, that is not a belt. That's a fancy rubber band with a buckle."

My mom put me in a ballet class, and all I could think about was what was for snack. "Yeah, yeah, plié, give me some *pud-ding*. When's Snack?" I was most excited when it was cheese and crackers, two of my favorite things. I loved the outfit, but I really didn't want to do the whole ballet part. So, my mom decided, "Okay, judo." Sigh. I was a strong little cookie, so I think I injured two kids. My mom said sayonara to the judo. I knew I was bigger than my peers, but I didn't give it much thought. I was in the safe bubble of my family, the baby girl who had the coolest toys.

Afternoons we would visit Mark at the bar, when all the lights were up. I remember its distinct smell, a blend of cigarettes, alcohol, and old leather. The scent of grown folks' cologne and perfume. We'd have lunch and Phillip would pester Monica until she'd hit him, and then she'd be in trouble. My sister was always blamed for Phillip's mischief or messes he made. We all joke about it now, but Monica was the whipping boy for the actual boy in the family. In his father's eyes, Phillip did no wrong.

We sometimes went camping on weekends with Mark and his friends in the navy. The image that many people have of Japan is the skyscrapers and bright lights of Tokyo. But on those weekends, we would drive to a beautiful, lush campsite near where a river ran wide into a valley. To get there, you had to drive up the mountain and then down the other side. It was steep and the roads were narrow, like the dive drop of a twisting roller coaster. But that never bothered Mark. What bothered him was my mom's reaction to his driving so close to the edge every time.

"Mark," my mom would hiss. He would ignore her, and go even faster to prove a point or just get the ride over with sooner. Inevitably, after he lurched too close to the cliff's edge or had one too many swerves to avoid crashing into an oncoming car, my mom would reach her breaking point.

"Mark, stop the car."

He would continue to ignore her.

"Mark. Hello?" she said, looking straight at him. "You are not driving my children on this road."

It was always the same routine: he'd stop short so we lunged forward, my mother sputtering words as she got out of the car, ripping open the backseat door to shepherd us out. Phillip wanted to stay with Mark, and would even try to get in the front passenger seat. Mark peeled off as soon as we were out.

If Mark's driving was dangerous, it was just as scary to walk along the road down the mountain. But this mountain forest seemed like a fairyland, with giant cedar trees blocking out the sky. In the spring, cherry trees exploded in color, leaving blankets of pink and white on the ground. Mark would wait for us, parked where the road leveled off, and then he would begrudgingly take us the rest of the way. Once you were in the valley, the river created a clearing, and the sun shone down on us as we began setting up the tents. Immediately, Phillip and Mark would go off fishing for rainbow trout. That was their thing. The campsite had a fish cleaning station, and they would make a big show of gutting and cleaning their catch. Monica and I would go off where the river bottomed out into a clearing and jump off rocks into the water. We'd swim with our sneakers on because the rocks were so jagged. The water was very cold, but you got used to it. I'd float on my back, looking up at the woods around us for as long as I could. Afterward, we'd hang up our suits and change into warm clothes to sit by the fire as my mom made campfire goulash in the biggest pot you've ever seen.

Just as it started getting dark, we were given bottle rockets to shoot from empty beer bottles. It was thrilling to me at five and six years old, that unmistakable *ziiip* sound as the rocket sparkled up in the star-filled sky over the river.

By the time I was seven, I was jealous of how much attention Mark paid to Phillip. On one of the camping trips, I decided I was going to go fishing with them. I had watched them so many times, I knew what to do, so I sat by the river's edge with Phillip's cane pole.

I knew you had to keep the hook just on or over the water so it looked to the fish like a fly skimming the surface. The trout jumps for it and gets caught. I caught one after just a minute or so, and it was such a surprise I almost let go of the pole. I handed the fish to my brother, afraid of the hook and afraid of hurting the fish.

"Throw it back," I said.

"No way," said Phillip.

I remember turning back and seeing something that looked like pride in my dad's eyes. I was just as hooked as that fish.

I caught seven rainbow trout that day, handing each to Phillip or my father, who joined in. It was such a special moment, because Mark was actually talking to me and even seemed impressed. I didn't see my own accomplishment; I saw my father's reaction to my accomplishment.

"Good job, Chrissy," he said.

I remember that day so clearly because that was the only time he gave me a compliment. I know that our perception becomes our reality, but I've given this a lot of thought. I am sitting here trying so hard to find one single moment like this. And I come up empty.

THANKFULLY, MY GRANDMA CAME TO LIVE IN OUR HOUSE IN JAPAN.
My mom's mom, Mary Lou, who I called Grams, was always made-up, and she left a light cloud of Elizabeth Taylor's Gardenia perfume on me with every hug. She wore huge sunglasses, with her hair kept short and tinted a slightly redder shade than her natural color. Almost as soon as she arrived she got a job at the Estée Lauder counter at the base commissary, doling out beauty advice. She looked like she knew what she was talking about, and she backed up her wisdom with kindness. Her repeat customers called her Obasan, which is a Japanese term of endearment for an older woman. Grams's go-to was coral lipstick and a great eyeliner, which is now my go-to. I would watch her getting ready for work, running her skinny brush through her hair, the hard bristles pulling her look to perfection.

I was already perfect to her as I was, so she never once gave me advice on how I should look. I felt so safe and secure with Grams that I would often spend the night in her room just to feel more of her love. I went to a kids' school on the base, and every single day she would come pick me up to make me lunch at home. All through kindergarten, lunch was always grilled cheese, the best you've ever had in your life. She cut it into two triangles, and she would put them corner-to-corner on the plate. My brother and sister liked it cut into four triangles, but two pieces looked bigger to me. Even then, I was beginning to associate fullness with safety and contentment.

Our relationship wasn't one of those where she spoiled me with gifts or material things. She was just someone who was happy to see me when I woke up in the morning. I didn't worry that my affection or my smile wouldn't be returned because someone was in a bad mood or, as I always thought, I had done something wrong.

People in my family would sigh and say, "Well, you're her favorite." If I was, it might have been because she saw how much I needed her. I was lonely with my brother and sister being so much older than me. I had only one real friend, a girl who lived next door who we all called Punkin. Grams and I might have had more in common than anyone knew, since she was probably lonely too. She'd left my grandfather, though she was too devout a Catholic to ever divorce him. He moved on with another woman, but for twenty years, she was on her own.

She understood men, and could give her son-in-law a look that said she knew exactly who he was. In turn, Mark was always a little intimidated by her. One time my parents were arguing, having a huge blowout in the living room. Grams came out of nowhere and stood between them.

"You're not gonna treat my daughter in that way," she said, stopping time.

It was one of those Wonder Woman moments where I realized I was part of a line of strong women. Grams, my mother, and my sister Monica are the strongest women I've known in life. I think even the strongest women forget how tough they really are sometimes.

As I understand it, my father was not faithful to my mother throughout their marriage. It was sometimes hard to deny. Like when Grams was at her Estée Lauder counter one day when a reliable customer came up.

"Obasan, I saw Mark buying that beautiful necklace for your daughter," she said. "Did she love it?"

"Oh!" Grams said, playing it off. "I will have to ask."

The necklace never materialized. I hope the woman he gave it to was thrilled.

"We're moving back to Florida," my mom simply announced one day. It was the first time "we" meant just my mom and us kids. Mark wasn't coming. He got an assignment in Diego Garcia. Yeah, I never heard of it either. It's a tiny island, a ring-shaped coral reef in the middle of the Indian Ocean. My parents were about as far from each other as they could get.

The family lore goes that on the very same day the divorce was finalized, Mark married a woman named Judy. When he was back in America and living in Miami, he invited Monica, Phillip, and me to camp out with his brother Tom and my cousin Tom (Big Tom, Little Tom). It was the summer before I turned nine. Judy was there, but nobody introduced us.

"I got this for you," she said, handing me an art kit of primary-colored paints in a plastic container.

"Oh, I love art," I said, trying to be nice. She went back over to Mark and smiled at him as he put his hand on her lower back.

Who is this bitch? I thought.

Not my mom, I answered myself. I wouldn't see my father again until I was twenty-one, at a shower for Phillip's baby boy. It was at Phillip's house, and Mark walked right by me in the family room. Even my high school graduation announcement came back Return to Sender.

WHENEVER I GO BACK TO GAINESVILLE, I STOP TO LOOK AT THE house my mom first found for the four of us. We lived there when my parents were just getting divorced, and when Mark was giving my mom money. It was a proper house, with three bedrooms, *two* bathrooms, a living room to play in, and a kitchen that seemed huge to me at the time. My mom could bake, and I could help without being told I was in the way. I missed Grams, who moved into a retirement home in West Palm Beach when we got back to Florida. She was a four-hour drive away, but she sent me cards and I wrote letters. We would each sign them *XOXO*. I missed seeing her every day, but she did her best to stay close.

When school started, the principal said I had to repeat kindergarten to make sure I had mastered the curriculum, since I had gone to school in Japan. I took that to mean I wasn't smart enough to be a first grader. But in a way, it was a fresh start. Even though my parents were divorced, I distinctly remember thinking, "This is like normal." We had a house and we even had pets. My brother had a ferret, which escaped, and we had a pet tarantula named Charlotte. Normal people had pets, I told myself.

Then normal just dissolved.

My mom couldn't afford the house and we moved into an apartment in what others told you, if you gave them your address, was "the ghetto." Our home was now a cramped two-bedroom in a single-level box of tan bricks. I recently asked her how much child support she got from my dad. "It was a hundred dollars a month," she said. "And it wasn't always consistent."

She worked as a checkout girl at the Food 4 Less supermarket, and Monica and Phillip got home later from school than me. So, I was a latchkey kid in second grade.

The first time I saw the red tag left on the door I didn't know what it meant. The apartment was old and always seemed dark anyway, and now the lights wouldn't turn on. I went to turn on the TV. Nothing.

Our electricity was shut off a lot. In Gainesville, there's a thunderstorm practically every day. I was alone in the dark during a strong one. After that, I just didn't want to be alone, period.

Every day I would go to the grocery store and just walk around. This one was a bit fancier than Food 4 Less, and I would pretend I was shopping, playing the part of the discerning customer. I loved the brightness of the place, and the feeling of being safe.

I spent so much time there every day that I knew the order of the Muzak playlist by heart. It was one long string of '80s power ballads. Wham!'s "Careless Whisper" would lead to Laura Branigan asking "How Am I Supposed to Live Without You?" I looked at all the food my family could never afford. I visited Capri Suns, which all my classmates had. I brought the cheaper juice drink in the plastic grenade-shaped jugs in my lunch bag. Oh, and the chip aisle, stuffed with bags of air and goodness. Real Doritos, not the fake "taco chips" we ate.

But mostly I just wanted to be around people. The supermarket staff ignored me, probably because I looked away each time they turned to me. I was so afraid of getting kicked out. I respected that they were putting up with me. "What is wrong with this girl?" I imagined them saying to each other. "Is she stealing?"

Never. First of all, if my mom found out she would kill me. It would be an insult to her pride. Second, it just never really occurred to me to shoplift. I befriended older kids in the neighborhood who even then I knew were a bad influence. They cursed and had their own bikes, casually doing loop-de-loops around me as I walked. They would steal from the Lil' Champ, the tiny convenience store near our house. I was the kid who would find a dime or a nickel and save up to buy Lemonheads. They were the cheapest candy, so I grew to like them. Let's be real here: I really liked chocolate. But Lemonheads were better than Now & Laters. They weren't enough Now for me.

My mom soon met a guy at work, Evan. He was quite a bit younger, but he was so kind. He came over one time and made us dinner. It was this casserole of cream of mushroom soup and rice with bacon-wrapped chicken. That exact recipe has stuck with me. We all sat at the table and he served us. He even asked me what I thought of the meal.

I was eight that summer, and like all summers in Gainesville, where it's never below 90 degrees, we spent as much time as possible at the springs. Back then you could pack up a whole car and pay ten dollars to get into Blue Springs. Now it's ten dollars a person. Blue Springs shoots off the Suwannee River. It is a shimmering, crystal-blue work of nature, with a dock right over the deep springhead hole, where the water is extra blue. When you go, and you should, everybody's in their bathing suits and having their picnics. People put their watermelons in the water when they arrive so it will be nice and cold when they're ready to slice it. Blue Springs is still the definition of summer to me.

It was May, and I remember walking up the ramp to the dock with my mom and Monica, who was fifteen. My feet crunched on the AstroTurf stapled to the dock to keep you from slipping off. I was in front of them, and suddenly I heard Monica scream at my mother.

"You're *pregnant?*"

I turned, and my mother reflexively touched her stomach. I don't know if Monica guessed from my mom's tummy in the suit. But I knew from my mother's face that she was right. She was pregnant. I felt my world crumbling. Standing on that dock, I instinctively jumped, raising my hands overhead as I crashed into the water.

As I sank, fear and uncertainty overwhelmed me. *Wait, my mom can't take care of us,* I thought. *She can't take care of me.*

And as I rose back to the surface, kicking my feet, my fear hardened into anger. I was too mad to even look at her. This was going to be one more thing I couldn't talk about.

My mom told Evan and that was the end of him. His mom, a woman named Kitty, got involved and demanded my mother have an abortion. She moved Evan to Michigan or Minnesota; either way, it was Siberia to Gainesville. Kitty worked at Jo-Ann Fabrics, where my mom bought the cloth to make crafts, clothes, and comforters. After our beautiful sister Morgana was born, we kept going to Kitty's store. Did my mom think that if Kitty saw Morgana she would want to help? Maybe. Kitty might have hidden in the back room when we came in, because I only remember seeing her one time when my mom and I went in with Morgana. Kitty looked at us, her whole face a sneer. She turned and walked away. It was heartbreaking to see that this person wanted nothing to do with this sweet little baby, her own granddaughter. My perfect little sister Morgana, who today is one of my best friends—someone I don't even want to imagine myself not having the gift of being able to talk to.

It wasn't long before we lost the apartment, too. The last night we spent there, I lay in bed, my hands clasped on my chest as I stared at the ceiling.

"What is happening to us?" I said to the dark.

MY MOM WORKED SO HARD TO MAKE THE RENT FOR THE MOBILE home in the Arredondo Farms trailer park. Our trailer was a single-wide, about eight hundred square feet, with three small bedrooms and a bathroom. I started my third elementary school in three years in Gainesville, and on the walk to school every day I stopped at the horse pasture next door. It was about ten acres of green, with four or five horses. I had friends who could afford to bring carrots along for the walk and we would feed the horses in the pasture. I loved them, and I made up a name for each horse.

We were lucky to have the beauty of Gainesville all around us, no matter how poor we were. Gainesville is one of the most magical places on earth, with a little bit of city and so much country. I love that you can still live down a dirt road and grumble about finding snakes on your carburetor. And as kids with no money, we could spend whole days exploring. Monica, Phillip, and I would go for hikes and get lost in the woods. One time in late summer, we must have walked through all of the northwest part of Gainesville.

We just kept walking. It felt like we were in Narnia and we would never get home. Even when the sun started to set, I never was afraid, because my big brother and sister were there. I only knew they were freaking out when we stepped into a clearing and realized we had wandered into the field of Monica's high school. "Okay," she said, in obvious relief. "Okay, now I know the way."

At night, we three played flashlight tag throughout the whole trailer park. When you get tagged by the light, you're "it," count to twenty or so, and then go to tag someone else. The secret to staying hidden is to keep moving, but I always gave myself away by laughing. Am I the only person who perpetually has to pee when playing Hide-and-Seek?

We were happy.

This was around the time my mom started going without food to keep us fed. Between tending to Morgana and her work schedule at the store, I think it was easy for her to hide this in the beginning. But one time we were all eating chicken and rice together and she just sat there with water.

"What about you?" I asked her. "What are you gonna eat?"

"Oh, I'm just not hungry," she said.

I didn't believe her then, and I admire her strength in doing without so much to keep the family together. The stress took a toll on her. I think having a clean, orderly house was a way to impose order on all the chaos of our lives. My mom was very meticulous about how she cleaned because it was something she could actually control. She made sure we were presentable and in clean clothes. We learned to scatter like roaches sometimes when she came home from working at the grocery store. There was a way she slammed the car door that told us she was going to come in guns blazing, looking for something wrong. The trailer wasn't a nice place to live, and it was important to her that we all do our part to make it look as nice as possible. If you put the dishes away incorrectly, she would pull them all out of the cupboard.

"Do this over!" she would yell. "Do it right this time."

If she saw a bit of clothing coming out of the drawer of the dresser, all the clothes would be on the ground.

"Refold everything," she would order. "Start again."

When she finally left Food 4 Less and started working at the University of Florida in the Contracts and Grants department, it seemed like my mom was getting on her feet. But the stress only seemed to show more. Of course, you think things like this are your fault when you're a kid. I don't remember spending a lot of time with her because she was working, and when she wasn't, I just felt like I was always in the way. Monica and Phillip would babysit, but they were teenagers who didn't want to be around a kid. I felt alone.

My mom had so much on her plate and didn't have the help of a partner, or really anyone. She was always cute and quick with a joke, so guys noticed. Soon after getting the job at the university, she started dating a man named Paul who had a comb-over and glasses. I didn't like him. When I was about ten, I came home from school to find he was trying to get my mom to do mushrooms. Anyone who knows my mother knows that was not gonna happen. After that, I absolutely hated him and wouldn't talk to him. Another time I came home to find them messing around. I heard the sounds you don't want to hear and fled. It just made me feel weirded out, so I decided once again that I would never go straight home after school. I played outside or went to my friends' houses, where they had better snacks or cooler toys. Or steady electricity.

I feel bad about that now. My mom was around the age I am now and she deserved companionship. She deserved to be sexually active and have pleasure and feel fulfilled. But our family life was so erratic that small issues could be disastrous. One morning there was a huge thunderstorm. I asked my mom if she could drive me up the road to my friend Christie's house so I could get a ride to school with her and her dad. My mom had a brown Corsica hatchback. Somehow, she drove through a wide puddle and the car stalled out.

"Dammit, Chrissy!" she said, hitting the wheel with her fists. "How am I gettin' to work?"

It started up later when it dried out, but I still felt like I had made my mother's life hard. I had made a point to stop asking her for anything, and look what happened when I did. Look what was happening because I was a burden who simply existed. Everything was my fault. All of it.

Monica dropped out of high school at sixteen to help take care of Morgana. It felt like another bit of order and certainty falling away. And yet her sacrifice seemed practical in the moment. What else was she supposed to do? I cannot imagine the weight of the responsibility on my sister. Monica is one of the toughest people I know, a person who uses all that strength she has in the service of love and family. The second I think about what she did I immediately start crying, so bear with me. It's tears of gratitude, but also tears for the loss of her normal childhood.

I know now that when families are in crisis, kids blame themselves, and kids also take on adult burdens. Which is why it is important that I say something else: Arredondo Farms is still there and I won't say a single bad thing about it. People look down on people who grow up in trailer parks. I get it; there's a stereotype. But if you are a young person living in one now, or just a person who is made to feel that your surroundings are not good enough, remember that your soul is what matters. Your body is a vessel for your soul, and what surrounds that vessel, whether it's a mobile home or a brown Chevy Corsica hatchback that stalls out in the rain, is nowhere as important as what is inside you.

three

TOO MUCH
BUT NOT ENOUGH

My mom went dancing one night with my aunt Debbie, my father's brother's ex-wife. I suppose they had a lot in common. They went to a tiny club at the Holiday Inn. And that night, with Aunt Debbie as her wingman, my mom met Trigger.

Trigger was a childhood nickname from when he had been obsessed with *The Roy Rogers Show* in the 1950s. Trigger was the name of Roy's horse, and he told my mom that as a kid he thought Roy was named Trigger, causing his family to tease him. "The name stuck."

Trigger had a good job with Coca-Cola and seemed stable, which is what Mom needed. He lived with his daughter, Rebecca, in a small, single-story, cinder-block house on a dead-end road in Gainesville. Monica was living in a tiny studio with her boyfriend by now, and Phillip had moved down south to Miami because my mother simply couldn't control him. She ultimately begged for Mark's help, and for once, he came to the rescue. So, my mom, Morgana, and I moved into Trigger's house a year after my mom met him—right in time for me to start third grade at another new school. I don't blame Rebecca if she resented us for infiltrating her house and felt like we stole her daddy away. She was Phillip's age, sixteen, and get this: Rebecca and my brother had dated before my mom and Trigger even met.

I know it's the South, but you can't make this stuff up.

I was just excited to be in a real neighborhood again. I remember feeling the same way I did in that first house we moved to after the divorce: *Finally, we are going to have a really cool life. Things are going to be okay.*

It was, but it wasn't.

Trigger had a lot of rules. One was that he had to be served dinner first. If my mom put any of our plates down before his, he would simply refuse to eat. I remember how angry he got when she made that mistake once. He threw the entire plate of food against the wall and stormed off. He also decided I was fat and lazy, so he created a chore list just for me. Wash and dry the dishes—quietly, he didn't want to be disrupted while watching TV—sweep the driveway until there was not a leaf in sight, clean the bathroom, take out the trash . . . anything he could think of to keep me busy. He said it was to give me a work ethic. To him, I was a problem to be solved. He would say about Mark, nodding in my direction, "*He's* not around." He had to raise the child the other guy had abandoned.

My mom married Trigger at the courthouse. None of us went. Soon my mother was pregnant again, with another beautiful girl she named Abigail. Thank goodness they didn't go with the other name they were thinking of, Jubilee. Trigger loved having his two biological children in the house, and was even welcoming to Morgana. Me, not so much. Trigger seemed to resent my existence; I couldn't do anything right. He worked from four in the morning to three in the afternoon, so it felt like he was in the house all the time I was there. My mother was always at work, so she didn't see how he treated me.

In the living room, I would sit with my arms crossed over my body, trying to be as invisible as possible. "Sitting Bull," he and Rebecca called me. I knew he hated any noise I made, but if I was quiet, he would demand, "Why are you so quiet?" If I hid in my room, I would hear, "Why are you wallowing in there?" He pronounced it "wallerin'," comparing me to a pig flopping in mud. "You're lazy. You ever gonna get up and do somethin'?"

It was as if he hated to have to even look at me. My body seemed to offend him, but he couldn't help but stare, especially when I was eating. Trigger and Rebecca joked about putting a lock on the refrigerator door. We had lived with a lack of food in the house for so long that when it was there, I felt like I had to eat it before it disappeared again. I discovered that food gave me a comfort like nothing since Grams made those grilled cheese sandwiches for me. Food was something to look forward to. My only happiness.

I was constantly nitpicked about anything I did, but I couldn't let Trigger ruin this for me. And so, I began to hide my eating. I'd get up in the middle of the night and eat. I'd sneak food from the kitchen to eat in the bathroom. I meet people who say, "Oh, I felt so bad that I ate a dozen bagels." That's never been my problem. It wasn't that I ate a lot, it was *what* I ate. Cookies, chips. Things I could eat as fast as possible to avoid detection. Things that would give me the brief bliss of numbness, and take my mind off what was going on around me.

My other secret joy was entertaining my sisters. I had a boom box, and would record interviews with them like a newscaster. They were young, so their answers to my questions were hysterical. As soon as we recorded ourselves, we would immediately play the tape back and fall on the floor laughing.

One time, we were all in the family room watching something when Morgana got bored.

"Chrissy, do the voice," she said.

Everyone looked at me, so I pretended not to know what she was talking about. I just wanted to fade into the background.

"Do the *voice*!" she said again.

So, I did, presenting the beginning of the evening newscast. She howled, and both Trigger and my mom smiled at me. For that moment, I actually felt good.

It became a thing in the family, with them asking for the impressions I'd picked up of actors or people we knew. I loved entertaining, and the feeling I had all over me when I could make them happy. I think I was trying to figure out what joy was.

I DON'T REMEMBER WHY TRIGGER HIT ME THE FIRST TIME. I KNOW HE thought I'd had it coming for a while. I bet I was too loud putting away the dishes. Or I didn't put his Coca-Cola in the fridge and he wanted a cold Coke. That would usually do it.

He never punched my face. Just my body, the thing that offended him so much. He shoved me, slapped me, punched my arm, and yanked my wrist. He would hit me if he thought I looked at him wrong. Whether there was a warning depended on the situation. Like if I didn't say, "Yes, sir."

"You did the driveway?" he'd ask.

"Yeah."

He'd be up and towering over me in a second, slapping my arm as if he were trying to revive a dead person. And then he'd grip where he'd hit.

"What's that?" he'd yell.

"Yes, sir."

He'd squeeze harder. "I didn't hear you."

"Yes, sir."

But mostly he hit me over things he imagined I did. I remember being on the kitchen floor after he knocked me over, and I was literally begging to know what it was that I did. He just shoved me hard with his foot.

I convinced myself that my mom simply didn't know what was happening, or just how miserable I was. I believed that if she could see the abuse, she would stop it. Then Trigger went ballistic on Morgana over something while my mom was in the house. She stopped him, insisting, "You will not do to those girls what you do to Chrissy."

So, she did know.

I was heartbroken. In that moment and in the years after, I felt neglected and unimportant. Even when I heard her acknowledge what was being done to me, I told myself she just didn't know the extent. Because if she knew how much I was being abused and tormented, she would leave. It wouldn't be enough that Trigger didn't drink and he was a good provider. But I was afraid to tell her. Because I was afraid that she really did know. And stayed anyway.

Looking back, I can see she made a difficult choice, and I can't judge her for it. My mom had a toddler and a baby, and she knew what would happen if she was on her own.

She had started over after the divorce, and then again with Trigger. She didn't think she could do it again.

I wanted to tell Grams, of course, but I didn't want to worry her more. She didn't visit us anymore, and I think it was because she had an aversion to Trigger. "It'd be so nice if you could live here with me, Chrissy," she said. She was on Social Security and living in a retirement home, so that was a dream. Monica had spent a month with her, and it had been this big secret that if revealed, would get her kicked out of the retirement home. But I would have loved to have someone happy to see me again.

To get away from the physical and emotional warfare, I spent as much time as possible at friends' houses. One of my best friends in the neighborhood, Michelle, lived about a half-mile away in the subdivision. I just loved her mother, Evelyn, too. She's passed on, and I still cherish her kindness. She used to drive us to school every day in her station wagon so we didn't have to walk. Michelle was always finding a reason to be embarrassed by her mom, like we all do with our mothers, so she would sit in the back while I sat shotgun next to Evelyn. When I went to Michelle's house after school, Evelyn would make us a tray of brownies and split it down the middle.

"Okay, Chrissy, this is yours," she would say. "And Michelle, this is yours." She would give us a gallon of milk and walk away. No judgment. For the record, Michelle wasn't heavy and no, we weren't doing something wrong by wanting to eat more than one brownie. Michelle's mom did whatever it took to make her daughter happy. It was the absolute opposite of what I saw at home.

My friend Liberty lived on the next street over, and I escaped there constantly. Liberty was and is a goddess. She was taller than all our friends, with long blond hair, tanned skin, and big boobs. We all wondered how it was possible for her to even have boobs in fifth grade, much less such big ones. She was part of a hippie family, and everything they did was just cool. Liberty went to a private school that I felt was super cutting edge. Her sister had Down syndrome, but we didn't see that, or care about it. Most of all, I remember that there was so much peace in their house. So much love. The kicker was their parents had divorced and had found other people, but they still would all visit and hang out with each other! I would watch them be kind and loving as one big unit, and I would study them like they were some rare tribe. This is what love is? When you coexist peacefully with other people? Where you strive to be the better parent? Where you put your own pride aside? I am so blessed that other families showed me what was possible.

Liberty's house had two windows and a long cement porch in front. We made menus and played restaurant. One window was the pay window; the other was the pickup window. We would drive our little bikes on the cement, not but three feet wide, to get our pretend food. We also offered table service, and you could dine in or out. We were fancy!

We did a lot of the ol' Slip 'N Slide, because that's what you do in the South. Especially if you don't have a pool, or didn't have permission to go to Westside Pool, which was our local cool-kids' hangout. If you're like we were and you can't get a Slip 'N Slide at the Toys "R" Us because it's too expensive, no worries. You just get yourself a big blue tarp, tie that thing down with some tent forks, and get you some Dawn dish soap. And hopefully you don't break your neck or a friendship by hogging turns.

Our neighborhood had a sort of hilly area and a creek that went all the way through. When it was stormin'—that's what we called it—which it always was, the creek would fill up. We'd put on our water shoes and get inner tubes. Now, this wasn't a great idea. First of all, this was not a safe creek to be in because who knows what the hell was in the water. On top of that, we didn't know what that creek emptied out into. I still don't know, to be honest. But we didn't care. It was so much fun—when you're a kid you're not afraid of anything. Well, maybe only adults.

One of the best parts of going over to people's houses was their VHS collections. (Mark had taken his with him.) I had two friends I used to watch *The Little Mermaid* with over and over again. We would assign roles to sing . . . Let me be clear, we *tried* to assign roles to sing, but the girls would literally have tear-your-hair-out wrestling fights over who was going to be Ariel. She's a courageous babe, so I get it. But I eventually realized Ursula is where it's at. Hell hath no fury like a woman scorned. Layers. She is complicated, y'all.

Any movie musical I could get my hands on, fuhgettaboutit. Whether it was *Grease*, *Annie*, or any Disney production, I knew every word by heart from sheer repetition. Singing became my way out. I would sing anywhere I was, especially if I didn't want to be there.

I found myself leaning toward the complex supporting characters of these musicals. I liked Stockard Channing's big *Grease* moment, "There Are Worse Things I Could Do," and all of her one-liners. She was privately sharing a deep secret of shame with the audience, trying to prove her worth. I understood what it was like to be so misunderstood. I mean, Annie is a cute, adorable girl with great songs—don't get me started on "Maybe"—but I wanted to be Carol Burnett as Miss Hannigan. When she drunkenly hiccups through "Little Girls," she is just so much fun to watch. You could believe she was really this crazy woman and not a caricature of a drunk. To make others believe that I was another person entirely, *that's* what I wanted to do. Maybe because reality was too hard on a fifth grader. For the record, I still quote all those movies like every day with my sister Monica.

School was another escape from the torment of home. I was teased about my weight at school, but it was still better than what I heard at home. It was a place where I could get positive attention. In fifth grade, I was nominated for Safety Patrol, alongside my friend Dustin. He was my birthday buddy at school, and it felt cool to share that day with someone who was already considered one of the hot guys. You got nominated to Safety Patrol for being responsible, being on time, and having great attendance. You either helped in the carpool lane with drop-off and pickup or you stood outside the younger kids' classrooms to make sure they arrived safely. The best part was that you got to take a big Greyhound bus to Washington, DC, at the end of the school year. The only bad part was that you had to wear this neon-orange belted sash. I was so embarrassed because it really wasn't my color. Oh, and it was way too tight.

When we went to DC, Dustin's dad was a chaperone. Neither Trigger nor my mom could afford to take off work. I adored Dustin's father. I thought, *I want him to be my dad.* Jack Pearson, my faux father on *This Is Us*, reminds me of Dustin's dad. He was strong, kind, funny, and made you feel safe.

It's about a thirteen-hour drive to DC from Gainesville, so we stopped at a Morrison's Cafeteria for dinner. If you're from the South, you'll remember that chain. We stopped the bus and a homeless person tried to get on.

The driver was real polite, and just said, "This isn't a public bus."

The guy got angry and started yelling, still trying to

board. Dustin's dad calmly marched right to the front of the bus.

"You can't come in here," he said, "We're on a school trip."

The guy turned to get off the bus, but then out of nowhere he reeled back and punched the windshield, putting a slight crack in it. I was so used to explosions at home with Trigger that my body seized up, waiting for what would happen next. Dustin's dad didn't react with violence. The guy simply walked away, and Dustin's dad shook his head. He had compassion for this homeless person who'd acted out of frustration.

Even so, we were all so impressed with Dustin's dad for protecting us that we created a song about him that we sang the rest of the way to DC, and all the way back. That was what it would be like to have a dad. To be a kid that someone protected. I didn't miss Mark, because there wasn't a relationship to miss. But I knew I didn't have anyone like Dustin's dad looking out for me.

I WAS FOCUSED ON WHAT I DIDN'T HAVE, BUT SOMETIMES THERE are moments where you think you have no choice, yet it's the best choice.

In the fifth grade, we had to choose from a list of famous people and give details about their lives. There were people like Princess Diana and George Bush who went fast. I was the last to get to choose and there were only a couple of people left. I saw a female tennis player who didn't look like the other tennis players I'd seen. She didn't look to me like the female athletes I knew from TV, little gymnasts and ice-skating princesses. She had cool glasses, and she wasn't smiling to be pretty—she was smiling because she looked like she'd just won something.

"I'll be . . ." I said, stumbling over the name, "Martina Navratilova."

"Why would you want to be her?" somebody said.

"I don't know," I said. "She seems rad."

"She's gay," some boy said. "She likes girls, you know. Are you a lesbian?"

"What?" I don't think I even understood the concept of gay or lesbian at that point.

"Who cares?" I said. "She's a badass woman who can kick ass." I looked at her photo again. She looked strong. Like she could take you down if you tried to hurt her. If she saw Trigger raise a hand at me, she could stop it.

I researched her in the school library to learn about her life. I wore as much white as I could for the autobiography speech, and I borrowed a sweatband to wear on my head. I'm still mad that I couldn't find a real tennis racket.

"My name is Martina Navratilova," I started. "I am the greatest female tennis player of all time. When I was eighteen I defected to America . . ."

It was exciting to play the part of a badass in front of everyone and to be unapologetically strong without fear of being punished for it. My classmates didn't really get it, though. They still assumed the last choice could never be the best choice.

The universe again intervened when I decided to join Band because all the cool kids were in it. And those cool kids all had money for instruments. My mom couldn't afford a rental fee for an instrument, so once again I was stuck with no choice but the last choice. The school's only spare instrument was a baritone horn, which is sort of like a mini tuba. All my girlfriends were playing the dainty piccolo and the clarinet, and I've got this big-ass baritone. *My big behind does not need to be carrying a tuba*, I thought. I was not gonna be the whomp-whomp punch line at the concert.

The Band and Choir classes were right next to each other, and I hadn't even considered Choir because at my school, none of the cool kids were joining it. And I really wanted to be cool. But one day after school, I was lugging that giant baritone to Band practice when I heard the most beautiful sound. The singers harmonizing and blending to make one voice spoke to me. I could be part of that. It would be like singing along to all those VHS-tape musicals. I put down that baritone and found my voice.

From the start, Choir was great. I needed it because it allowed me to express myself but not have the full focus on me. Besides, at the time, I didn't think I could sing well. I loved to sing, but I know now that the way we sing reflects the way we see the world, and I was wounded and scared.

I know that might surprise you to hear now. Not because I am a great singer, but because I simply don't stop. Should we call it a gift or a compulsion? People say "Hello" to me and I am suddenly singing Adele or Lionel back to them. Either one is appropriate. It's as if I have a constant loop of theme songs, jingles, classics, and the latest pop hits running through my mind at all times. I just now started singing Willie Nelson's "Always on My Mind." True story.

It's funny that I sing today with such joy because the universe handed me a baritone. I was lugging around this heavy thing, thinking, *Of course this is what I get.* And of course, I have last pick at presentations, just like I'm picked last in PE. I was misunderstood and mistreated.

The whole time, the universe was conspiring for me in ways I couldn't understand, certainly not back then. I was getting what I would need for my journey.

AND SOMETIMES THE UNIVERSE GIVES YOU PUBERTY. NOT SURE PUberty was a joy for anyone, but I always felt like I was too much or not enough, and puberty amplified that. I loved swimming, and during a Florida summer you just live in your bathing suit. It's too hot to put clothes on, plus if you're swimming you can't tell if you're sweating, Hal-le-lu! But girls started wearing bikinis and shorter and shorter jean shorts unbuttoned at the waist. I became so aware of my body that I was too embarrassed to wear my bathing suit, even with a shirt on. I didn't have a cute swimsuit because they didn't make cute swimsuits for my size.

I remember looking at my friends' bodies thinking, *How?* They were developing curves, and I felt that wasn't gonna happen for me. I was just chubby and round. In PE, all the other girls changed in front of each other, while I changed in a stall.

I never wanted to draw attention to my body and always wore oversized clothing. I wore a lot of collared fake Izod and Lacoste-style shirts. All my friends would share clothes from stores like Wet Seal, but I could only share accessories. For me, it was, "Um, can I wear your necklace?" Because, well, it fit.

What I really wanted was a pair of forest-green Umbro shorts like all my friends had. It was the team color of our school's Westwood Whirlwinds, so everyone got the same pair of nylon shorts with the checkerboard sheen. I wanted them so bad, asking and asking my mother until she finally got me a pair.

I tried them on at home and the material was not giving one bit. My thighs strained against the nylon until the seams began to rip. I was heartbroken and simply hid them. I started wearing long shorts made for men.

There I was in a fake Izod shirt and men's shorts, just as other girls were reaching puberty and owning their sexuality. I had a different crush every hour, but I began to see how our guy friends would look at my girlfriends, playing Spin the Bottle and those kinds of middle school games. I was definitely the girl who was friends with all the guys. I always heard "You're hilarious," and "You're so cool," but of course, none would want to date me because of how I looked. So, I became a darn good matchmaker. I got to be a spy in both camps.

"I know who you like," I'd say to a cute boy, my voice obscene with flirtation. It was a way to relate to people. If I couldn't play the game, I could at least coach it.

I knew I would be a great girlfriend—despite everything Trigger told me and did to me, I had an inner voice that told me, "I know that I'm a great girl. I know that I'm a good person. I'm fun and I am kind."

My friend Callie had that thing that made all the guys like her. She was adorable but a bit of a brat. In the seventh grade, she called me one night and said, "Chris and I are gonna hang out at the church on the corner. You wanna come?" The church was just up the road from my house, and Chris was a really cute soccer player with curly hair. Tall and kinda quiet. So, I said yes, because, you know, *boys*.

When I walked up, they were sitting across from each other in the park behind the church. "We're gonna play Truth or Dare," Callie said.

I rolled my eyes. "This is what you dragged me here for? You can't play Truth or Dare with Chris by yourself?"

"Shut up," she said. "You're first."

"Okay," I said. "Truth."

"No," she said. "You have to say Dare."

"No, I don't—it's called Truth or Dare," I said. "It's not Dare or Dare."

"No, I want you to say Dare."

"Fine, Callie. Dare."

"No, no," she said. "I want you to say Truth."

I think I mentioned already that she was a brat. "Fine, Truth. I don't care."

"Okay, so it true that you like Chris?"

I gave a look that the very idea was ridiculous. "Uh, no."

"Yeah you do."

"Okay, if you say so," I said. I turned to quiet, handsome Chris. "But I don't. No offense."

You and I both know I liked him. Of course I liked him. But I wasn't going to say it. And I assumed he liked her—everybody liked her.

Callie didn't even give Chris a choice of Truth or Dare. "I dare you to kiss Chrissy," she told him. The way she said it, she knew he wouldn't. She just knew there would be no way he'd want to kiss *me*. Everyone's last choice.

"Okay," he said. Nonchalant. Just like that. Okay.

"What?" Callie said.

Oh God, oh God, oh God, I thought.

"Are you ready?" he asked me.

"Whatever," I said. "It's your dare."

He leaned toward me, and at first I didn't close my eyes, because I was afraid he was going to fake me out. And then it happened. Chris was kissing me. I was having my first kiss. I closed my eyes. His lips were so soft, and he smelled like a boy, all grass and sweat. Then I felt it—the softest, nicest tongue ever created. Okay, it was the only tongue I had experienced to that point, but it was perfect. Now, I didn't say I knew what the heck to do with it, but it was happening.

"Okay," Callie said. "*Okay.*"

He acted just as nonchalant afterward, but some-where . . . somewhere in the depths of his soccer player soul, that boy liked me. I knew it. Even if he was too ashamed to admit it. I was certain of it. And if he did, other boys might, too.

say thank you

Do you have ten seconds? Not for me, but for you? I need you to set aside ten seconds every single morning. Maybe that will increase one day. But for now, I just need ten seconds. My hope is for you to come to find yourself in a constant state of gratitude. I pinky-swear you'll be happy you did. I can say this because I know I was resistant. Imagine that, huh? I just couldn't—or didn't want to—believe setting aside seconds would completely change the rest of my day and my life.

Here's how I do it: Before my hands automatically reach for my phone, I close my eyes and I take these ten seconds for my daily practice of thanksgiving. I think, *I am grateful that I can see.* Just saying that makes me appreciate the light filtering through the window, no matter how early my call time. I thank my bed for its support and comfort.

I am grateful to have the ability and mobility to move my miracle of a body. Down to the organs' functions, it works perfectly on my behalf. And then there's the fact that I can move freely and easily, in my house with running water and electricity.

These seem like small things that we all take for granted, but they're key. Through my daily practice I have come to find that my attitude is gratitude. I don't always start with the same acknowledgments, and not every morning is the same. I have had days I wish I could start over, but I still try to keep myself focused on giving thanks.

Here's my challenge to you: When you wake up in the morning, do not get out of bed until you have focused on at least five specific things for which you are grateful. Do this as soon as you wake up. Don't check your socials; don't even think about looking at your emails. This is an active meditation, where instead of blocking out thoughts, your mind is rich with all these wonderful gifts. Some of you may want to create a gratitude journal, and that's fine. But I want this practice to be something you can do wherever you are, and on the fly. For instance, if you find yourself at a complete standstill in traffic, take a moment to appreciate the pause. Relish the freedom you have to drive a car. Enjoy the company of your carpool friends, or great music on the radio. I never want this to feel like homework.

Ideally, this practice sets the tone for your mind-set and, in turn, your day. I did say *practice*, which means we are trying to acquire proficiency. No need to beat yourself up if you jump out of bed one day and forget. When I sleep through my alarm or hit the snooze for the third time, I run around like a madwoman making excuses. But I've come to find that when I take that time for myself, I am more patient, more understanding, and much more loving.

I guarantee you that doing this will make a difference, because I know what happens when I miss it. I don't feel as empowered. I don't feel abundance in my life. I think that's because you can't give from an empty well. When you don't realize how full your life is, you can't give to others. And when you cannot give to others, you will not be able to receive.

How often do we take the people closest to us for granted, the same way we do our eyesight or the magic that makes a lightbulb turn on when we flip a switch? The very things—or people—we take for granted are what we should be most thankful for. The quiet, ordinary times are more extraordinary than we give them credit for. The moments that we get to share.

So let me say to you: I'm so glad you're here.

four

SECRET SUMMER

The summer before ninth grade, I was trying to figure out who I really was. Puberty had magnified all my issues of feeling like I wasn't good enough, and now I felt even more different from my friends. And at home I was constantly picked on for who Trigger *thought* I was. To stay out of his sight, I spent as much time as possible at my then best friend Mya's house.

As her friend, I was expected to keep up with the drama of Mya's relationship with her boyfriend Ethan. There was always some new development. They were like grown-up married folk.

And Derek would be there.

Derek was Mya's brother. He was a couple of years younger than me, but had swag for daaaaays, swag that made him seem so mature. Then he would do something gross that reminded me how immature he was. But all that could be forgiven because he was so. Incredibly. Hot. He played baseball, so naturally I would sit there and just watch the muscles of his forearms flex and ripple. He had an awesome tan, and Mya told me once that somewhere down the family line they were part Native American. All I knew was that this guy had the most perfect color skin, had perfectly shaped lips that hugged the sides of his beautiful teeth when he smiled, and his chocolate-brown eyes danced when I said something funny. I was always trying to make people laugh, but his genuine attention and interest was everything to me. That moment of his joy, from something I caused? That was life.

I slept over at Mya's on most weekends and often ate dinner with her family during the week. They always sat down at a table, and we never did that at home. They had a routine. They made time for one another. Mya barely ever went to my house. I sort of kept my home life off-limits to her and all my friends. If we arranged to all walk somewhere, I would have them meet me at the top of the street. I don't think anyone thought that was weird, or if they did, they never mentioned it. I couldn't handle seeing how people reacted to our tiny house, full of unfinished projects and mismatched paint. Besides, whenever Trigger was around my friends, he would be nicer to those friends than to me, and I didn't trust him not to make fun of me in front of them. To cheapen me in their eyes.

Ethan lived in another town, and his parents would

drive him halfway to Mya's house, then Mya's dad would pick him up and drive them back to Gainesville. I knew they were having sex, but the fact that Mya didn't make a big deal about it made them seem light-years more grown-up than me. Ethan would kiss her whenever one of them was leaving the room, even just to get a snack. *That is a real relationship*, I would think to myself.

Mya and Derek had two little sisters they were expected to watch, so the crew all just hung out together. We'd ride our bikes to the store or walk around the neighborhood until we'd have to run in the house from the afternoon rain. The radio was always on, and we'd either listen to country music or turn on VH1's Top-20 Countdown. Sometimes we'd put on a movie. I think that is the very adolescent PG version of "Netflix and Chill."

One day a bunch of us were crammed in the living room waiting for the storm to blow over. Derek was sprawled on the couch, his arm slung over the side. I watched him as Mya told some story, and I marveled at how some people just had no problem taking up space.

He turned his head from Mya and looked right at me. And his eye twitched.

Almost as if he winked at me.

Did he have something in his eye? I looked away. Of course I looked away. I didn't want to make him feel awkward because I felt awkward. Because of course he didn't just wink at me.

A little while later, I got up to go use the bathroom. As I passed him on the couch, his fingers ever so slightly raised so that they gently brushed the outside of my thigh. I didn't look down. I walked into the bathroom, my eyes bugging out. I closed the door and turned to the mirror. "Whaaat?" I said as quietly as I could yell. I stared at my own shocked reflection and did what normal people do: I started asking myself questions in the mirror.

"What just happened?" "Did he do that on purpose?" "Did I imagine it?" From shocked, I went on to mug about three different looks. Happy, shocked again, then completely affronted by the brazen nature of this naughty, bold man-boy. I decided it was all in my head. If he did mean to touch me, he was almost definitely doing it to be cruel. While I was in the bathroom, he was probably telling everyone what he did to make me look and feel like an idiot. "Watch Chrissy," I pictured him saying to our friends. "Watch her now. She thinks I like her."

I walked back into the living room, taking care to be out of his reach. I wouldn't look at him. I was looking at everyone else to see if he had involved them in the joke. No, they were all just talking, no one even looking my way.

I sat back across from him, and he again looked at me. He smiled, an unmistakable grin of conspiracy. *What do I do now?* I didn't smile back, though I wanted to. I was afraid to look stupid. I mean, what if he wasn't really looking at me? I tilted my head in what I thought was a noncommittal, knowing look. His smile broadened.

There was a slow build over the next few weeks. The winking continued, and the excitement consumed me like I was Baby in *Dirty Dancing*. He became increasingly nervy, pointedly staring at me while we were all in a group. The second anyone looked at us he looked away. I put some mental and emotional notes in my diary, and I may have doodled our names a bit in there, still not sure if I was an object of desire or absurdity.

Dinner at Mya's was once my safe place, but it became part of the game. As soon as everyone was passing the meat loaf or vegetables, Derek would blow me a kiss or lick his lips.

He did not! I would scream in my head. Homeboy was livin' on the edge.

I loved it. But I always questioned why.

Before bed at one of the sleepovers, I left Mya's room to get some water. He was in the hallway. As I inched by him to get past, he pulled me toward him and put his hand on my butt.

"What are you . . ."

"Meet me in the living room after she falls asleep," he said, his face close enough to kiss me. Oh my God I wanted him to kiss me!

I gave him the what-the-hell-are-you-thinking look I had perfected since he began all this flirting.

"Just do it," he said. "I'll be waiting."

"Okaaay," I said as my heart nearly beat out of my chest and my conscience quickly paid a visit. Did I mention it was a quick visit?

You and I both know I wanted this to be real. It seemed like it took Mya forever to fall asleep that night, and as she talked about how much she missed Ethan, I did a terrible acting job of pretending to fall asleep. Eventually, around midnight she began the lightest snore. I gave it a bit, staring at the ceiling, moonlight filtering through the blinds. Would he really be there? What if he was just setting me up to make fun of me?

I crept out of Mya's room, into the hallway, and past their parents' closed door. I could see light coming from the TV in the living room. And there was Derek, turning to look at me as if he could feel me there.

"I couldn't sleep," I said, acting as if we hadn't planned this. "I didn't want to wake Mya up," I added to sell the excuse.

He smiled and nodded his head toward the couch next to him. I sat down. We watched a ridiculously bad cartoon; I think it was Ren & Stimpy. Wait, who am I kidding? I don't even know if the TV was still plugged in. We kept looking at each other. I could feel an electricity between us that warmed my entire body. I casually put my hand palm-up within reach of him. Just putting my hand out there, in case anyone wanted to, you know, hold it. Or not. He had to make the first move, and then I would know he wasn't just teasing.

He did. Derek reached his hand over and took mine. *This is love*, I thought, trying not to shake. *This is the feeling.* I was so in the moment, and my whole life was that hand in his, being held. He gradually sidled closer to me, and then brought his other hand up to my face to pull me in to kiss him.

Let me tell you, my first kiss with Derek was—to this day!—one of the most amazing kisses, if not the best ever of my life. It was slow and sensual, as if he'd perfected a Hollywood kiss over years of training. But, like, how and with who?

We kissed for a while, and the intensity outweighed my fear of being caught. Eventually, we slowed down, and I was afraid we would fall asleep cuddling on the couch. "Hi, kids," I imagined his parents saying, finding us entwined. "What did you want for breakfast? Eggos okay?" Not gonna happen.

We got up and went back to our rooms. He kissed me again at Mya's door like it was the end of a date. I decided it was. I lay down on the floor and thought, *Now I know what love is.* I replayed every moment, turning the whole experience this way and that to examine it. He reached out for *my* hand. He pulled me in to kiss *me*. He wanted *me*.

He slept in the next morning, so I didn't see him. I was exhausted but had to go home to do Trigger's chores. As

I swept the driveway, cleaned the bathroom, and did the dishes from the dinner I missed the night before, I thought about Derek. Cinderella had a prince.

Sort of.

The next time we were all at Mya's, I followed his cue. I waited for him to acknowledge me in a real way, not just through his secret signals. When he didn't, I decided we had a secret. This was what I needed to settle for—a wink here and there. He couldn't let anyone know he liked the fat girl. Got it.

The "dates" continued during sleepovers at Mya's. I never once went into Derek's room. The fear of being caught was exciting for both of us. Once I was in the family bathroom, brushing my teeth before going into Mya's room. He slipped in and with the door wide open, he stood behind me in the mirror and began rubbing my thighs.

"Exscushe me," I said, through a mouthful of Crest. "Oh my goth."

I bent to rinse my mouth, then looked up at us. *Us.* He smiled.

"Okay, this is too much," I said, laughing. "I can't."

"See you later," he said.

I lay on Mya's floor, thinking about our secret. It got to a point at every sleepover that I couldn't wait for Mya to fall asleep. "I'm tiiiiiired," I would say. "Let's go to bed. Aren't you ready?" I couldn't wait to be in the living room with Derek, kissing and loving the feeling of being bad.

We would keep the TV on as cover if we got caught, but he would just be paying attention to me. When we talked, we talked about music or I would do impressions of Jim Carrey's characters. I would hear something on television and later be able to re-create it for him. He wasn't just the best kisser; he was the best audience.

By early August, poor Mya, in whom I used to confide everything, had become an afterthought. Time with her was the toll I had to pay to be alone with Derek.

"Mya, I can just sleep on the couch," I said. "I feel bad crowding you."

"No, it's okay," she said.

"Really, it's fine. I don't even need a blanket . . ."

"Sleep in my room with me!" she yelled. "What is the point of a sleepover then?"

"Okay, fine, I will."

Of course, I wanted to tell her what was happening. Especially since I was planning my wedding. I had found the one person in the world who was actively attracted to me and not some boy kissing me in a game. I had to make this work. I wanted Mya to be the maid of honor, and I pictured her giving the speech. "Now we are sisters," she would say, gazing at me sitting with Derek at a little sweetheart table. "I am so happy for you." Sometimes I would lose myself in thinking about going on a double date with Mya and Ethan. I'd be a normal teenager, walking around the mall or going to the movies with my best friend and our boyfriends. There was a flaw in the plan: Derek. It became clear when I got too comfortable around him in front of our friends. Meaning I said, "Hi, Derek."

He curled that perfect upper lip I loved and looked away, exhaling in a mix of disbelief and disgust. The night before, he'd kissed me with those same lips and told me I was beautiful.

Another time, Mya and I were going to walk to the supermarket. "You wanna come with?" I asked him.

"Why would I want to do that?" he said, too loud. So loud even his friends gave him looks. "Why are you even talking to me?"

I started to cry, and played it off as someone being randomly mean to me.

"My brother is such a dick," Mya said as we walked.

"Yeah, he is," I said in a quiet, defeated little voice. "I don't know why."

I wish I could say I ended it there or even called him on it. But I was still so hungry for positive attention and what I'd settled on being love. I held on to the connection between us, and this pocket of time where we could be together. It was easy not to talk to him about how he hurt me, because by then I had started my pattern of acting like things simply weren't happening. I stuffed my feelings with food. And that's how I handled it.

In September, I started ninth grade while Derek was

still in middle school. *That is not cool*, I told myself. *Even if he wants to date openly, I am not dating an eighth grader.* Starting at Buchholz High was excruciating. My house wasn't zoned for the school Mya and all my friends were attending. I was so miserable and all alone. In middle school, I had earned a reputation as a Funny Girl, something that I thought would eclipse Fat Girl. But there I was the Fat Girl, with a couple of friends I rarely saw.

I remember getting in an argument with one particular girl in the bathroom the first week at this new school. There were four mirrors and four sinks, and I was washing my hands at one of them. This girl, trying to be as intimidating as possible, came up behind me.

"You need to move."

"There are four mirrors," I said. "*You* can move."

I don't think anyone had ever stood up to her.

"Oh, it's like that?" she said.

I was just tired. People were constantly making me feel I was doing something wrong. My mother, Trigger, and Derek. And now this girl, saying I was at the wrong sink. Something in me broke. She was Trigger telling me to put the dishes away quietly for once, or screaming at me for leaving a leaf on the driveway. She was one more person telling me I was taking up too much space. If this was going to start happening at school, that would leave absolutely no place where I wasn't in somebody's way.

I looked at her in the mirror.

"Yes," I said, "there are other mirrors you could be using."

"Okay," she said, smiling. "Okay."

Instantly I was cool with her. I'd stood up for myself.

I wasn't ready to do that with Derek. When we saw each other, it felt great at first, but it always turned sad. Each time I hooked up with Derek, I told myself, "That's the last time."

And then it was. I was hanging out with everyone at the house on a weekend in late November. His guy friends began to tease him about someone in his class.

"Nah, Derek likes Lisa," said one.

He gave them a smirk, then looked at me.

I looked away. I wouldn't even look at him. I was terrified of him thinking I was hurt or that I was dumb enough to think we were a couple. Instead, I sulked and wrote bad poetry about heartbreak.

I didn't feel safe showing vulnerability, so I did it all alone. It's ironic, because now showing vulnerability is all I do in my work. I could say I didn't trust anybody, but really, I didn't trust myself. The one time I chose to show up for myself in all that time was about a sink. How could I expect other people to do something for me that I wasn't willing to do for myself? I made it acceptable for Derek to keep me secret, because what alternative was there? I didn't think I was worthy of being claimed.

I moved on. Which means that I would be walking

along and think of him, and the floor of my heart would drop and I'd feel empty inside all over again. So I ate more. I grew to a size 12, which at that point made me the heaviest girl in my grade. And I became one angsty teenager. I was dealing with so much pain that I turned it into anger to survive.

Mya got an old '86 Honda when she was fifteen. She didn't have her license, just a permit, so technically she needed to drive with her parents. She was dating a new guy then, Garrett. She wanted to visit him and since I was spending the night, we took a little adventure. We got into her car at midnight and snuck over to her boyfriend's house.

Garrett's mom found us all sitting in the living room. She was a schoolteacher and she brought the wrath of God down on us.

"Why are you here so late?" she asked.

We all shrugged.

"How did you get here?"

I remember that before she drove us home, she made us write apology letters to our parents because we were so unsafe and irresponsible. Every teenager's gotta have that experience at least once, right?

My friendship with Mya slowly dissolved for no apparent reason, as teenage friendships sometimes do. But my friendship with her meant so much to me. I learned a lot from the time we spent together, and of course, her family gave me something I didn't get at home—a safe harbor.

I recently heard from her stepmother that Mya is happily married to her new wife! How amazing is that?!

Derek echoed through my life. Some of those thoughts were good, some bad. I wouldn't feel worthy of love, or able to remotely trust a man, until I was in my mid-twenties.

About five years ago, I went home to Gainesville for Christmas. I went to the Oaks Mall, the one mall in town, to go shopping for Christmas presents. I was walking by the Santa setup over by Belk department store when I saw a man with four kids. He was covered with tattoos on his arms and neck.

He looked familiar, and I asked myself, *How do I know him?*

As I got closer, I looked right at him and he just smiled. One knowing smile encapsulating all that time of me longing to be his.

" 'Sup," Derek said.

"Hi," I said. I had frozen Derek in that summer. Now he had gold teeth and overplucked eyebrows, and he looked older and worn out. He was going to be in the minor leagues. He was going to be this cool, hot athletic guy. The one that was too good for me.

"How are you?" he asked.

"Good," I said. "You?"

"Good."

And we kept walking away from each other. I turned around to take one last look. I wanted to say a million things.

I wanted to ask if he was ever in love with me way back then. If he could have taken me out, would he? I wanted to ask what happened to him. Was he happy now?

Instead, I kindly wished him a Merry Christmas.

He smiled. "Merry Christmas."

As I turned, I thought how much I had loved this man-boy. How I had pinned all of my dreams on him. *Maybe he's not the one that got away*, I thought.

Maybe I am.

five

BE NOT AFRAID

He'd get the scale from the bathroom and clang it hard on the kitchen floor.

"Well, get on the damn thing!" Trigger would yell. "This is what you need to know."

When I was fourteen, Trigger began weighing me. I never knew what would prompt him to get the scale. He started doing it out of nowhere, and then it became what felt like on a daily basis. There was no way of telling when the humiliation would happen. The only thing consistent was that he wouldn't do it while my mom was around.

When I heard that clang, I had to stop whatever I was doing and come to the kitchen. He sat in a chair next to the scale as I got on. Before he even bent to look at the number, he'd be shaking his head, disgusted at the sight of me. "You need to know this," he said. And when he did look at the number, he'd recoil in disbelief.

"*Good God almighty!*" he yelled every single time. I was with him recently and he said that about the price of something. I was right back in that kitchen, praying.

Good God almighty.

The number then was about 140 or 130. I knew I was a big girl at fourteen, and that most of my friends weighed about ninety pounds. The number on the scale didn't bother me as much as the interrogation and berating that followed.

"Why are you getting fatter?" he demanded. "Are you drinking my Coke?"

"No," I said, leaning with a hand on the counter, waiting for it to be over.

"What are you eating? You gotta be eating *something*."

"Nothing."

"Then why are you just getting *fatter*?"

"I don't know."

I look at pictures of me from that time, and I would be so fine with being that size now. But I thought I was gigantic. By then the beating had escalated. He had it in his head that I was trying to get between my mom and him. He would accuse me of doing drugs and sneaking out to have sex with boys. I was petrified of any of that stuff. There were things my stepsister did that I took the fall for. I didn't want to tell on her, and anyway I knew there was no convincing Trigger that I hadn't done anything.

Trigger would take my bedroom door off the hinges, convinced I was hiding something. Eating, or doing drugs—I don't know. He would just unscrew it and cart it away. "You don't need no damn privacy!" he'd yell. This would usually accompany a grounding over something he thought I did. If I came in four minutes past curfew, I would be grounded four days.

One time he hit me, and I just sat on the couch willing myself away. And I looked at him for once. I looked right in his face. *If I had a gun,* I thought, *I would shoot you. I don't want you to live.*

Afterward, I was so upset with myself that I'd thought these things. How could I think that about this person I loved so much? Because I really did love him. This man did more for me than my father ever did. He was smart, and I was allowed to quietly join him in watching the Ken Burns *Civil War* documentaries on public television. The ones with the dramatic readings of the letters home. Remember those? "My Dearest Anabelle . . . The days and weeks pass and I long to be near you . . ." They get you. Even Trigger. I remember looking over and seeing a tear in his eye.

"God almighty," he'd say. "Gets me every time."

I nodded. "Me too." I liked these points of connection. I clung to them because I needed to figure out why this person could do right by me as a provider, but be unable to love me. I got into Gator football and baseball, and we'd watch the games together with our boiled peanuts and his chewing tobacco.

But always there was the sense that I was an unwelcome guest in his home. My mother was stuck in the middle, with this man providing for her two small children and a daughter he couldn't stand. One night when I was fourteen they had a huge fight, which was blamed on me. And they came up with a solution.

"You have to go," Trigger told me. "You gotta get outta here." The solution to me not fitting in was that easy: I needed to not live there anymore. I remember the moment I realized my mother wasn't saying no.

"What am I supposed to do, Mom?" I asked her. "Where am I supposed to go?"

"Call your father."

It was as if she suggested I make a wish. I didn't speak to Mark. "I'm supposed to call him?"

"Yeah," she said.

I slid down onto the threshold of my room, which was naturally doorless at the time. She handed me the cordless phone and gave me each digit of his number, which I punched in like I had never used a phone before. Halting, searching for each number through tears.

I hoped he wouldn't answer so I could say I tried. But he did. I still couldn't call him Dad, so I just said, "Hi, it's Chrissy."

There was a pause, so I barreled through it. "Trigger says I can't live here no more."

More silence. I looked up at my mom, standing over me with her arms crossed.

"She says I have to ask." I paused. "She says I have to ask you to take me."

The response came so quick. "We can't," he said. "We can't have you live here."

"I don't have anywhere to go," I said. "I can't stay here."

"Well, you can't be here either."

That was that. "Okay," I said. "I have to go."

"Okay," he said.

I hung up. I told my mom, "I have nowhere to go. I don't know where you want me to go."

She walked away from me. *She's siding with Trigger,* I thought. I cried for hours in my bedroom and into the night. I know there are some people who have parents who drank, and they were used to the blowups that deflated once their mom or dad sobered up. Trigger didn't drink, and my mother lived on coffee and water. This wasn't an episode that would be resolved in the light of the morning. The threat that I had to leave loomed over me for years, a deep and painful secret I never told my friends. What could I tell them, anyway? I don't want to speak casually about abuse, but it had become so everyday to me that I don't know how I would have even explained it then to

Monica. She might have had some sense of what was happening, but I didn't think she could do anything about it. I couldn't exactly move into her tiny studio apartment with her boyfriend, so explaining the severity would just make her feel bad.

I still didn't tell Grams, but I think she knew things had taken a dark turn. "I really, really wish you could live with me, Chrissy," she continued to say. Maybe to give me hope, Grams sent more letters and prayer cards from her church. I felt a connection to my Grams when I looked at the paintings of people on the cards, saints like Theresa with her roses and the Virgin Mary holding little baby Jesus.

And so I went to church.

I STARTED ASKING MY MOTHER TO DRIVE ME TO HOLY FAITH, A CATH-olic church in Gainesville, every Sunday. I usually went alone, but sometimes I would take a friend or go with the friend and her family. I would always sit in the first or second pew.

Some of my friends were forced to go to church, so they didn't really get why I would happily go on my own.

"I like the music," I'd explain.

It's true that I did like the music. They sang traditional hymns at Holy Faith, which I loved because it felt so pure. There was one that I particularly loved because it was a favorite of my grandmother, "On Eagle's Wings." It's a hymn that reworks the 91st Psalm, which is basically a "You've got this" pep talk. I also loved singing "Here I Am, Lord" and "Be Not Afraid," which are songs of reassurance for when you're really going through it.

I would always say I went for the music because I couldn't tell my friends that I was searching for meaning and something greater than my problems. I sat there asking God, "Why am I going through this?" and "Why is my stepfather so mean to me?" You know, if everything happens for a reason, what was this for?

There was something comforting about the ritual of mass. Knowing what to do, when to stand, and when to respond to the priest in one voice like in Choir. As I genuflected, I sincerely prayed, asking for direction and asking to be of use. Grams sent me a prayer card with the Prayer of Saint Francis, and it remains an important prayer for me today, with my favorite part coming midway through:

> . . . let me not seek as much
> to be consoled as to console,
> to be understood as to understand,
> to be loved as to love . . .

Those Sundays were the beginning of my spiritual journey. My faith has taken different shapes, but that communion with others has always been a key part. For me, it's always about love. We're made from love, with love, to love.

I WAS SEARCHING AT SCHOOL, TOO, TRYING TO FIGURE OUT WHERE I fit in in that new place. And I admit that in the beginning I did a shitty job. Freshman year of high school I was on the defensive, mad about Trigger and hurt by Derek. I didn't trust a single person, and I thought that at any moment I was going to be hurt. I was holding a massive grudge against so many people in my life that I then projected it onto my classmates. Let's be honest, I was a bitch.

I would never start stuff, but I would finish it. A girl tried to embarrass me, saying that I liked some guy and it would never happen. I walked up to her, got straight up in her face, and raised my hand like I was going to slap her in front of everyone. Instead, I flipped her hair.

And then Kristen walked into my life and became my new best friend. Well, she was pushed. We had a mutual acquaintance who thought it was funny that we had the same shirt. It was a men's shirt, blue striped with all different shades of blue and gray. The sleeves were too long, and girls probably shouldn't have worn that shirt. It was kind of fate that we both wore it, because she was an average girl, not a big girl. She had thick, long black hair and we both had these bangs that curled in the constant humidity. Twinsies.

This was toward the end of that terrible year. And she became that one friend I needed to help me relax so that I could make more friends.

"Yeah, I was so afraid of you," Kristen told me recently when we were talking on the phone.

"*Why?*"

"You were just so tough," she said, "and you had this 'don't fuck with me' thing."

"Well, I was defensive," I said.

"Well, it worked."

I was so afraid of being vulnerable I almost missed out on a best friend. But I could be myself around Kristen. I could admit to her that I loved attention, and I could be zany and carefree. I always think that we're like the women in *Beaches*, where she is the smart, kind Barbara Hershey character. And I am like Bette Midler—"Just give me the stage!"

We were so inseparable that Kristen's mom used to joke, "You and Chrissy are always together. Is there something you want to tell me?"

"No," we would say in unison. We liked boys a *lot*. It just wasn't mutual. Boys didn't like us. The difference between Kristen and me was that she liked one guy the entire length of high school, and I liked a new guy every fourth period. The guy that she liked, named ST, was adorable. He was funny, and kind of goofy. He was a Boy Scout, and I know this for a fact because Kristen made me go with her to his Eagle Scout ceremony.

She never told him about her crush. Instead, she would get nervous around him every time. We had a Slam Book, which we passed to each other in class. If you didn't have one—well, you missed out! It is a spiral-bound notebook that friends pass to each other instead of notes on pieces of paper. So, you have this keepsake of all of your secrets. We wrote letters to each other in the Slam Book, and throughout the day I would get fickle about whichever boy I decided was The One for Now. But all our Slam Books were full of "I LOVE ST." All caps, 'cause girl was serious about her man.

As I got more comfortable through my friendship with Kristen, I was able to open up to other people. I am grateful that I can say I was friends with everyone. Cheerleaders, theater kids, the art kids, ROTC, everyone. My natural inclination is set to love, and I just got out of my own way. I could tell that everyone else was searching for who they were, just like me. It was still tricky, though, because I didn't feel popular. Not by any means. I wasn't an athlete. I would have loved to be class president or treasurer or something similar, but everyone in that crew was rich. These were kids coming to school in Mercedes-Benz Kompressors and I remember thinking, *What do you aspire to have if you have a Mercedes at sixteen years old?* I certainly wasn't getting a car in high school. My mom wouldn't even buy me a pair of Nikes.

So I got a job. At fifteen, I started at McDonald's, doing three to four hours after school and working weekends. I worked the back drive-thru, and yeah, I was a little resentful when the rich kids drove through in those fancy cars on their way home to do their thing while I stood there in my cotton uniform shirt smelling like French fries. Kristen got a job there too, so that was nice. She had her dad's two-door Nissan truck, so we felt very grown-up leaving at the end of a shift. It was a stick shift, and I was always impressed that at sixteen she could drive that thing. She was and still is fiercely independent.

The best part about working was that having a job seemed to give Trigger less to complain about. He was still very tough and verbally abusive, but I so craved his approval that I hung on to his begrudging acknowledgment that I was bringing in a wage. I was good at it, too. My manager was so nice that he inspired you to be the best employee, just for him. He was thirty, which seemed so old to me and Kristen at the time. He would generously compliment all the employees, which made us only want to be and do better. Imagine that. Positive reinforcement.

I saw the drive-thru as a chance to connect with people, even if it was for that eleven seconds. It was like a performance, where I could do off-kilter voices at the mic. On nights, I'd entertain with my English accent. Picture an Adele-type cockney accent with a touch of class:

"Welcome to McDonald's," I'd say, ever so grandly. And then when they saw me at the window they'd have this look of confusion.

"Hi, how y'all doing tonight?" I'd say.

"Wait . . ."

"Excuse me?"

"Never mind."

You gotta pass the time, y'all, so we tried to keep it interesting. My manager would always say, "Chrissy, if you're not in the back drive-thru, you have to be at the registers. We need you with people."

When I wasn't working, my high school choir director, Miss Rollo, would give me extra time after school. She really believed in me, or just took pity on me—whichever, I'll take it. Junior year, she volunteered-slash-suggested-slash-told me to go to a one-week choir camp at the University of Florida. She strongly suggested to them that I be offered a scholarship to attend. It was magic. There were music professors, and conductors, and professional singers. I remember sitting in a scat class thinking, *Oh my God, I love music so much.* But I looked around and there were people who were brilliant at sight-reading and could play every damn instrument. Performers who came out of the womb like Stevie Wonder.

Yup, not good enough, I said to myself. *Okay.* But I loved music, so it was enough to just be around other musicians and singers. It really provided hope for me, because I'd believed I was going to have such a limited life. My mom made too much for me to get full financial aid and too little to actually put me through school. These were artists who had come from Gainesville or been the square pegs in the round holes of their small towns, some going to college and some not. But they all seemed like they were doing what they wanted to do, not what they had to do.

All through high school, I had been afraid to audition for Chamber Choir. You had to audition and you had to be the best of the best of the best. I just wanted to hang out with these people, so I embraced my fear and auditioned for my senior year.

I got in, and it changed my life.

Before that, I always thought, *I'll just blend in.* Now I could do solos. Oh God. Why did I want to do solos?

We even went to State, where I performed a solo at the competition. The song was "The Lass from the Low Coun-tree." It's a beautiful song written by the folksinger John Jacob Niles. Since I liked performing so much, nowadays people ask why I didn't join Theater or do any high school plays. The answer is that I was just too damn afraid. I was afraid of not being good enough, and I let that fear get in the way of doing something I know I would have loved.

I had plenty of reasons to think I wasn't good enough. Or that I was too much to even look at. When I was younger, I was aware of being different and aware that people were in-tent on making me feel that way. I had to cover up, literally with shirts and long shorts, and emotionally by hiding my secrets. What made me stand out to people initially was my size, and it gave them the impression that I was not worthy, was lazy, or whatever people's perception of what plus-size is. And it's more than about size. I know now that at our core, we are all these perfect beings. But many of us are not taught this. Instead we are told, "You're not smart enough." Or, "You're not pretty enough." "You don't deserve the happiness you want." What I have learned is that hurt people hurt people. I have the honor of meeting a lot of people these days, and when we go deep as we share, I see how that truth, hurt people hurt people, resonates.

I recently met a woman in LA who didn't know anything about my childhood. She was a shaman, and I am all in when it comes to people exploring the essence of things. We were talking and she told me she could see me as a child.

"Did you spend a lot of time with your arms folded tight over your chest?" she asked.

I thought back to the living room in Gainesville, where Trigger would call me Sitting Bull.

"Yeah," I said.

"You were protecting your heart," she said. "You didn't want to be tarnished by other people's energy."

"Oh," I said. *Oh.*

"You were keeping something inside you safe from harm."

I have come to terms with my feelings about Trigger. He wrote me a letter when I first moved to LA that I have kept with me for more than thirteen years. "I just want you to know," he wrote, "that you do things I never thought I would see you do. You are so much more courageous than

I've been in my whole life." He talked about being hard on me, and he said he was sorry. And he said he loved me.

That's all I have ever wanted him to say. It's heartbreaking, but it's also why I am so sure everyone is put in our lives for a reason. I would not be who I am without all that I went through. I have had to grow to understand that I owe Trigger so much for doing what my biological father never did for me, and still acknowledge that he tormented me. It was Trigger who kept a roof over my head. It was Trigger who taught me how to drive and Trigger who took me to the driver's test. And he also made my life such hell that now, I feel nothing can break me.

It has been so hard to think about that time and share it with you, because I have never, *ever* talked about these secrets. It's hard not just to feel that pain again, but to realize that it is all still there, so close to my surface. I believe that pain is in every pound that is still on my body. I stuffed my feelings for so long, they must come up and come out for there to be a real healing.

And part of that healing was having an honest conversation with my mother. About a year before *This Is Us* started, I was with her in Gainesville. We had shot the pilot, and every day I questioned whether it would be picked up—or if they would replace me. You just never know. As people I'd never met decided the fate of the show and of me, I was in limbo. So, I had time to see my family. I went home to

Gainesville for five weeks and slept in my old room. I was forced to be alone with my thoughts and to view my childhood through the eyes of an adult.

One day I had just meditated when my mom appeared in the doorway. She asked how I was feeling, seeing as how emotional I had been for the last few days. I was dealing with a lot of anxiety, and I looked to prayer and meditation for solace. I felt as if something broke open.

I wanted to ask questions and finally express to my mom some of the pain I had been carrying around with me for the past twenty years.

"Why didn't you stick up for me?" I asked. "Why did I get treated differently? How come I was so often the afterthought?"

She told me the truth, and it's hers to share. I will just say this: I got a better understanding of how desperate she was to keep the family together. To not have her children separated and put into foster care. She endured her own struggles with Trigger, and she worked incredibly hard to hide them.

If I have Trigger to thank for testing my strength, I have my mother to thank for giving me her strength in the first place.

preschool rules still apply

I didn't go to college, but I sure did learn a lot about life teaching preschool. This was right after I graduated high school, and I was really excited about this job because it was at an elite preschool that had a cutting-edge approach to learning. Every day there were different electives, and I got to see my students take part in Music, Dance, and Art. It was hands-on and felt nothing like babysitting.

The kids were on average four years old and they hands-down were smarter than I was at that age. There was a boy named Daniel, who spoke so well. "Uh, Miss Chrissy? I believe I am a little damp," he would say when he wet himself. He always had me hollerin'.

But even if the kids were more advanced than I was at their age, there were still fundamentals they needed to learn. And since as adults we're all just big kids anyway, I truly believe there are lots of us who could use a refresher. So, here are a few of those preschool basics that I taught back in the day:

1. EVERYBODY HELPS CLEAN UP.

I was fortunate that I co-taught with one of the lead teachers, Miss Lynne. She was a wonderful woman. She lived way out in the country, and I remember she kept this animal bone that was wrapped in a mass of horsehair. She had tied a huge rubber band to it so that she could bob it like some demented toy. What can I say? Kids love creepy things. She saved that tool for when the kids were getting lax about the rule about cleaning up toys.

She had it behind her back at Circle time. "Kids," she said, "this is what happens when you don't clean the dust bunnies underneath your bed." And she'd bounce this hair-and-jawbone thing at the kids as they screamed in delight. "You gotta clean up!"

That did it. The kids jumped right up and began marching around looking for clutter. "We're gonna clean!" they said. "We're gonna clean! Clean up, clean up, everybody, everywhere!"

What I loved about this rule was that it kept the emphasis on the positive, which is a focus in preschool teaching and it should be in everyone's lives. The rule is not "Don't Make a Mess." That's unavoidable, either through your choices or mistakes. But you always have the power to clean up after yourself, and help others do the same.

I do this literally. I was at a Hollywood Foreign Press event the other day and I saw two empty champagne flutes stashed in the pot of a plant. I picked them up and looked for a better place to stash them. Someone said, "Chrissy, you don't have to do that." Yes, I do. This whole life thing is a group effort, y'all.

2. WORK IT OUT ON THE SPOT.

If there was a fight or a misunderstanding about a toy or whose turn it was to do something, as teachers we were taught to handle the situation right on the spot. That way, the children could communicate their feelings right away instead of lashing out later. "It hurt my feelings when you took my toy away." And the person then was given a choice of how to make things better right away: either give it back or find a way to share.

As an adult, that just doesn't happen. You move on with your feelings or you harbor resentment. We rarely really deal with issues in a rational way on the spot: "Hey, what you just did hurt my feelings. I want you to know." It feels awkward. It is too hard. But when you do, the person apologizes. Or maybe he doesn't, but at least it doesn't fester in your head. It's funny, because my biggest challenges at preschool were the kids who bit and kicked because they *couldn't* communicate their feelings. And that's what adults do. Maybe you don't bite the guy you can't stand at work, but you lash out. I truly believe a nasty "Reply All" is the grown-up's bite mark.

3. USE YOUR LISTENING EARS.

I can't tell you how many times I was able to get my students' attention with, "Okay, put on your listening ears." Sometimes I would literally act like I was putting on my own. We all know how many distractions there are in the world. I look at my phone and it's like the jukebox display of alerts for all the things that need my attention that instant. But a lot of that is just static.

The person standing in front of you, however, is not static. I see people acting as if they are engaged in full conversations, but they are checking their phones the whole time. They might as well be saying to the other person, "Hey, whatever is on this screen right now? Way more important than you."

So many people, including myself, talk at each other but don't listen. To ourselves or to other people. Believe in actively listening to yourself. Take time to have a conversation with yourself every now and again. What's working? What could maybe use a little tweaking? So often we're on autopilot and we slip into addictive behaviors to avoid listening to ourselves. We eat, or drink, or, yes, check our phones—anything to avoid hearing what we truly need to say.

4. DO YOUR BEST WORK.

This sounds so simple, but people seem to forget it early on. When you know you did your best on something, you can let it go. If you find yourself obsessing over some lost opportunity or a project that didn't go the way you wanted, being able to say, "I did my best" is like an insurance policy against regret.

In what I do, this is about preparation. If I don't make my responsibility my priority, I will feel ill prepared, and it stresses me the eff out. To memorize scripts, I physically write out my scenes again and again. I also use an app called LineLearner, which lets me record the lines of the people in the scene. I can selectively remove characters or remove myself, and I can run the lines.

5. WORRY ONLY ABOUT YOURSELF.

Oh honey, yes Gawd. You can become distracted by other people. The ones who are amazing on social media, juggling work and play, and doing it all with such grace. I don't even know if I have clean underwear today.

Worrying about yourself wasn't exactly a rule in preschool, but it's something that was effective in the day-to-day policing of childhood jealousies. Kids are obsessed with getting their fair share, and quick to point out when they think someone got the bigger snack, the better color, or the first turn. "How come she gets . . ." The answer that always worked was, "Worry about yourself." As adults, we sometimes call this the Compare and Despair trap, where you look at someone else's life and become envious or feel inadequate. We can't know what other people have gone through or what's really behind that Instagram post.

6. RAISE YOUR HAND TO SPEAK.

If you've ever been in a room full of children, you know that everybody has something to say that needs to be heard that second. And then there are the kids who are shy, who can easily get drowned out by others expressing—okay, yelling—their needs and feelings. Where do you fall? Are you sometimes waiting for someone else to voice your concerns or needs?

I was doing this video of a celebrity sing-along with a bunch of actors getting different parts of the song. I was told beforehand that I could choose any part of the song I wanted to sing, so I went with a chorus and a verse I liked.

When I got there, they said, "Oh, can you sing this part instead?" I didn't want to ruffle any feathers, so my first instinct was to say yes.

But I said no. Because I couldn't sing the part they wanted me to. And the world didn't end. There have been times I've regretted *not* raising my hand to speak up about something, but I have never regretted advocating for myself or someone I care about.

7. BE A GOOD FRIEND.

We would refer to the kids as "friends," as in, "Okay, give your friend a turn." So, it wasn't so much about giving Marcus a turn, but just about doing what was right for their friend. Also, the kids then grew to automatically consider new students friends on arrival. Parents told us that if they were at the playground on the weekends, they could invite kids that they didn't know to play with them by saying, "Friend, do you want to play?"

As adults, we sometimes have a guilty-until-proven-innocent approach to people. We make them prove their worth to us. But if we accepted newcomers to our lives as cool at the outset, and *then* got to decide if they live up to our openhearted expectation, I think we'd all be a lot happier.

six

YOU'RE HERE FOR A REASON

You never know when the universe is going to say, "Hey, Ms. Thang, you're not getting out of this one."

When I was twenty, I spent a lot of time babysitting my little sisters Morgana and Abigail. They were friends with another set of sisters, Jenny and Annie. Four preteen girls. Oh Lawd is right. Jenny and Annie's parents had to be out of town a lot, so I would sometimes spend entire weekends judging dance routines and stopping fights over whose turn it was to use the phone.

One day we were listening to the local radio station when the DJ announced there was an open-call model and talent search going on at the Holiday Inn in Gainesville. The same Holiday Inn where my mom met Trigger. The Inn is happenin'!

All four immediately started screaming, "Please take us! Just take us. Take us!"

"How do you know it's real?" I asked. "I'm sure they just want your money."

Morgana got in my face and looked right in my eyes. "Please, Chrissy," she said. "Please."

"Oh fine," I said. There may have been cartwheels.

We went, with Morgana and her friends all dressed up in what they thought models and singers wore. Morgana went into the audition room first, and I sat at the table outside to fill out the kids' forms because I was the boring adult for the weekend.

I looked up to see this woman sitting across the table. She was white, in her thirties, and had a sweet face. She had an interesting brown hat tilted to one side. But what I really remember, more than how she looked, is how she made me feel. Like she was waiting for me.

"I taught at Buchholz," she said. "I remember you."

"Oh, wow," I said, thinking, *No, you didn't, crazy lady. You did not teach at my high school.*

"Are you auditioning?"

"No, I'm just here for my sisters," I said. "They wanted to—"

"You are here for a reason," she said. "You should audition."

This crazy rando lady said it with such authority that I

believed her. It was a sort of validation of something I already knew but was afraid to admit. I deserved a chance too.

As I was mustering up the courage to grab a form to fill out for myself, Morgana came out of the room with the woman in charge of the talent search. The woman, this oncoming force of fiery red hair and brassy personality, looked right at me.

"Who are you?" she barked.

"I'm Morgana's sister."

"Uh-huh," she said, nodding. "So, what do you do?"

"Uh . . . uh . . ." In my heart, I was already singing in my Disney princess voice, *I want to sing and dance and act and do eeeeevvvverything!*

Instead, I just repeated, "Um, I'm Morgana's sister."

"Do you sing?" she demanded. "Do you act?"

"I would love to sing, but I . . ."

"Well, sing something for me."

"Uh," I said. "Oh dear."

I looked around and the woman in the hat was gone. I went someplace in my mind and I just started singing "Reflection" from *Mulan*. It's a song about not being seen, and also being afraid to show the world who you truly are.

As I sang, she cocked her head like she was impressed. "Okay," she said, cutting me off. "I'll be in contact with you before we leave Gainesville." She and her business partner were based down in a small town just south of Orlando.

When she called and told me she wanted to be my manager, I said yes immediately. Her focus was on placing talent with agencies in Florida with the hope of eventually getting them signed in Los Angeles. She told me I had to come down to Orlando, where she and her partner were going to host an acting class for beginners. I didn't count on that. First of all, acting hadn't even occurred to me. I thought she wanted to help me become a singer. There was also the drive. I was afraid to drive on the interstate—I'm talking white-knuckle scared—which is ridiculous, because honestly the road between Gainesville and Orlando is only two lanes.

"Chrissy, put your big-girl panties on and drive to Orlando," she said.

I did, and on the way down I wondered what the catch was going to be. When I got there, the acting studio was just a room you could reserve for free at the library. There were about twenty people there, and my manager and her partner had written scripts for fake TV commercials for us to do "cold readings." Cold readings are when you perform with little to no rehearsal.

I really didn't like doing the commercials. I had never done anything like this before. I didn't feel authentic. "Just be yourself," my manager said. "Just do what you think is the right thing."

It was my first legitimate time reading a script—someone else's words on a piece of paper. I was scared out of my mind. But I did my thang, which meant nobody was going to be buying anything from me. I decided it wasn't about the product, it was about the performance. I played the role as if I were the town drunkard or a Brit from "Souf London." I know, interesting motivation for selling soap.

"We're gonna have to start writing monologues for you guys," my manager's partner said. This was exciting to us, and so the next few times we met, the teachers talked to us about our lives and wrote monologues tailored to us. They were steering me toward comedy, and didn't seem to think singing was what I should focus on.

After a few months of three-hour classes, the managers felt our motley crew was ready for an agents' showcase in Florida. A manager sort of nurtures your career, and an agent procures the auditions. My manager and her partner made money coaching us and charging us for classes, then farming people out to Los Angeles and becoming known for having a great eye for talent. And they would also get a commission when actors booked gigs.

They created a piece for the show called "Inconvenience Store," and we all had different monologues. It was smart because they gave you ways to show different talents. I played the cashier, and as I was mopping up and talking to the audience, I sang Oleta Adams's "Get Here (If You Can)."

Our manager then auditioned the students to see who might be ready to represent at a talent showcase in LA. When I was picked, I was so excited! I had been saving up my money, so it was a big decision to gamble it all on this.

But something told me to. Trigger and my mom didn't object—they couldn't help with the fare, so I think they were just glad I could finance it myself.

This was going to be my first time in LA, and it was cool to just be on a plane with all my acting friends. We were an army platoon preparing for a *battle*. We'd be competing against other acting schools from all over the country.

I competed for Best Dramatic Monologue against at least one hundred people. The field would eventually be narrowed down to the top three.

My manager wrote my monologue based on conversations I had with her about growing up. She felt writing to our experiences was the best way to get authentic performances out of us, and she was right. She focused on my stepfather, drawing me out about the torment and the abuse I had experienced. The monologue was titled *Celine Dijon*, and my "character" had a stepfather who said she was too fat to ever make it as a singer. He called her Celine Dijon. It was frightening and freeing at the same time to describe some of these upsetting moments I had never shared. I had hidden my childhood trauma, but now I could share it under the cover of my character.

I came in second place in that competition, and it was such a huge deal for me. Something clicked—I began to envision a life for myself as an actor. I really thought I was going to be the female Jim Carrey. Like, who was writing *The Mask* sequel and when do we start shooting?

In December 2004, my manager asked me to officially become her assistant. I had been helping her out with all kinds of things for a while, but staying in Gainesville. The plan was that we would go out to LA for pilot season that January, and I would be her right hand as she and our respective agents tried to get me and six or seven young clients cast in network shows and commercials. When I gave notice at my preschool job, everyone there was excited that Miss Chrissy was going to go to Hollywood. I had a karaoke going away party, and my best friend Kristen and I sang "Wide Open Spaces" by the Dixie Chicks.

People ask how I was brave enough to make the leap to go out for pilot season, and the truth is that I was desperate. I was bored with my life, and I knew that if I stayed in Gainesville it would be a vortex I'd never leave. I might have also been in denial, because I don't think I fully understood that I was leaving Gainesville for good. It felt like I was heading to summer camp. I don't even remember saying goodbye to my family. I am not sure if this was denial at work, making it easier for me to leave my mom. I thought I would just help my manager by submitting the girls' head shots and taking them on auditions. All the actresses who'd be coming out to California with us were just beautiful—what by then I knew the industry called "marketable." I knew what that word meant, but I didn't understand how much size would play into casting until I actually got to LA.

THE MORNING WE LEFT, WE ALL MET UP IN THE GAINESVILLE DAYS INN parking lot. We were going to drive across country, caravanning in my car and two vans driven by grandmothers carrying their granddaughters to Hollywood stardom. I would drive Lia, who I think was fifteen, in my little four-door Focus, and my manager would switch in and out of all the vehicles, pitching in to help drive as needed. At twenty-two, I was the oldest of the actresses, with everyone else being under eighteen.

Our manager gave each driver a walkie-talkie so we could stay in contact. When she handed me mine, I thought, *Oh my God, I am going to drive across the* country? *Are you joking?* I had barely made the trip to Orlando, which was two hours of straight-up white knuckles on that interstate. This was a thirty-six-hour drive we were spacing out over four days! Who was this girl?

As we were doing the final pack-up, the Napiers drove up. They were a family with a daughter and son who were both great actors. I didn't know why they were there because even though they were joining us in LA for pilot season, they were coming out as a family in a few weeks. They all came up to hug me.

"What are you guys doing here?" I asked.

"We just wanted to see you guys off," said Mrs. Napier, "and let you know that we're gonna see you in LA."

Mr. Napier was kind of hanging back. He was a badass, beloved teacher at my old high school. We all just loved him—he was a great teacher and an incredibly kind human being. He suddenly turned toward me and handed me a wad of cash.

"What's this for?" I asked in surprise. It was 150 dollars or so. I knew my mother could never give me that kind of money.

"I don't know," he modestly responded. "In case you need it."

My eyes welled up and I hugged him again. I was so moved. I knew every dime counted in Los Angeles, and I didn't have many dimes. But it was more than the money.

Someone invested in me.

Finally, we all took off on I-10. My best friend, Kristen, made me a mix CD of jams, so I popped that in. Daniel Bedingfield's "If You're Not the One" came on, followed by R. Kelly's "Ignition." Lia and I did all the "beep-beeps" and the "toot-toots" on that one. As I drove, I became more confident. We got through Louisiana quick, but I remember Texas took forever. Halfway through I thought, *We should just turn around—we will never make it all the way through Texas.*

Eventually we stopped in a tiny town to eat. The whole place might have been one street. Our manager was in my

car, and she saw a shop that had a stuffed deer wearing over-
alls, sitting on a fence.

"Where in the actual hell are we?" I said.

"Oh, we *have* to stop there," she said. She loved antiqu-
ing and weird stuff. When we got out of the car, we noticed there was the lightest layer of snow on the ground.
It was like we had been transported to another world. The
shop was fun: really country, with a lot of hand-painted
salt-and-pepper shakers and plaids. I remember it smelled
like apple pie.

"Where you girls headed?" the woman sitting on a bench
asked. I guess this was a place people only stopped at on the
way to somewhere else.

"We're on our way to Los Angeles," I said. And one of
the other girls chimed in, "We're actresses."

"Stay safe out there," she said.

"Thank you, ma'am," I said.

I meant it. I felt like I was on a crazy adventure and
needed all the help I could get.

I learned so much about myself in those four days driving cross-country, going through different states and cities
that I'd never dreamed of seeing. At one point, there was a
five- or six-hour period when Lia and I were in my car and
the walkie-talkie stopped working. We couldn't get cell service, either. I had my eyes glued to the vans in front of us,
scared to death that I would lose them. Did I mention it was
raining buckets? I was there with this teenager counting on

me and I didn't know what part of Texas we were in. I was the responsible adult? Jee-bus.

But it was so much fun. El Paso for the best guacamole of my entire God-given *life*; San Antonio for a Bill Miller's Texas sweet-tea travel mug and some challenging civil engineering. The roads are just loops. Every mile took me farther from where I'd been and closer to who I wanted to be.

In Tucson, Lia and I got up early to pack, just in time to see the most beautiful sunrise. We had the radio on in the car as we waited for the others. John Mayer's "3x5" came on and he provided the perfect soundtrack. In that song, John's writing home to somebody he wishes could be with him as he travels. "You should have seen that sunrise with your own eyes," he sings. "It brought me back to life." As the song ended, I thought, clear as a bell: *Oh my gosh, this is the start of my new life.*

We could have slept through that sunrise. I would have missed the message. Just as that kooky lady at the talent search had said, I was here for a reason.

Because showing up for yourself is sometimes the lesson. It's only a failure if you don't try in the first place. When you put one foot in front of the other—get through one walkie-talkie-free mile after another—you cannot fail. Your dream might evolve. You might see that something isn't meant for you, and that realization will lead to what it is you are really supposed to be doing. But until you show up for yourself with that first step—because I know that is always the hardest part—you will never know. I had to get on the interstate to Orlando. And then drive cross-country. I had to conquer each fear so I could conquer the next fear. And the next one after that. Let me tell you, this wasn't easy, and it was something completely new for me.

If your initial response when you think about your dream is "No, I can't. I'm too scared of what might happen," that means you are afraid to fail. And if you are being honest with yourself, you might even admit you're also afraid of success. But whether it's the fear of success or of failure doesn't really matter. I think what it boils down to is that people are afraid of change.

When I was sitting in that car watching that sunrise, I was present. I wasn't worried about the day's drive, or how I was going to make it in Hollywood. I wasn't stuck in Trigger's kitchen, being weighed. I wasn't waiting for Derek to choose me. I wasn't hoping for my father to love me. I was just present with myself, and I was enough for myself.

It would be some time—we're talking years—before I learned the importance of staying present and not getting stuck by worrying about the future or lamenting what happened to me in the past. Acting has helped me so much, because you *must* stay present. You can't worry about the next scene because you're in one this moment. It's the same thing in our lives. Just play the scene and see where it takes you.

seven

THESE ARE
THE BREAKS

We couldn't contain our excitement when we crossed the border from Arizona into California. It was so *MTV True Life: I'm Going to Hollywood*. Every city on the road trip had had its own voice, and LA's was so big and loud that it made me speechless. There were all these cars and the freeway. Everything seemed intimidating and strange.

Our new home would be Kenwood Mews, which is an apartment complex off Hollywood Way in Burbank. Think *Melrose Place* with a random assortment of desperate hopefuls and a few working actors. We had a two-bedroom apartment and slept on air mattresses, with three girls in each room. Our manager slept on an air mattress in the living room. There was a plastic table with plastic lawn chairs, and the table was covered with our head shots and résumés, along with a printer, highlighters, pens, and pencils. Our little makeshift pilot-season proving ground. At night, we played Uno in between hoping for auditions, and all day we worked on scripts together. I would take the kids on auditions, wishing for callbacks and praying for the wild card.

In the meantime, we had to budget all our money. Vons supermarket was a quick walk to save gas money, and our go-to was chicken fingers. It's always supposed to be sunny in Southern California, but every day that winter it felt like there was a dang deluge. And thank God, because Subway had this Rainy-Day deal that if you bought a six-inch sub and a drink, you got another six-inch sub for free. First sign of rain, we'd haul boogie to Subway and get ourselves a free sammich.

At first, I was the driver, just taking the kids to auditions, and then as they booked gigs, I became what's called a "set nanny" because an adult must be present on the set for a minor. So many actors lived in Kenwood Mews that on my way in and out, I would always see packages of scripts left downstairs addressed to actors whose names I knew. I would think, *One day a script is going to be sent to me.*

But as the weeks went by, it felt more and more like no one was going to give me that chance. Yes, I had an agent, but that entire pilot season, I had two auditions. I didn't get either job. I had already lost fifty pounds before moving to LA, per my manager's suggestion, but it became clear to me that I should either lose more weight or stay the butt of the joke. Back then there were even fewer roles written for people of size. You were a size zero or a sight gag.

So how do you get a job without opportunity?

I had no idea, but I didn't give up, because I loved acting. How do you neglect something so firmly placed on your heart? I think when you stand out, and for me it's as a plus-size woman, you think, *How am I gonna do this? Do I—and can I even—conform? Why am I relegated to my dress size?* I had to stop caring about what I wasn't and focus on what I was. Courageous, committed, and willing to sacrifice for something I wanted. As an actor, I got to be another person, relate to her plight, and lean in with empathy to understand her how and why.

That's all I wanted someone to do with me.

People know it wasn't easy for me to make it as a working actor, so I am often asked for advice. All I can say is that you really must love it. Everyone's journey is different, but you have to have real passion. That's true for whatever your work is. Because that love is gonna get you through hard times and long hours and the "What am I doing with my life?" situations.

My manager wasn't paying me enough to live on and I rarely had auditions. By rarely, I mean twice. When my agent was looking for an assistant, my manager committed me without hesitation—or a conversation with me, for that matter. I was happy to have a real income so I could afford to get my own apartment with a roommate, which made the move to LA seem sort of permanent to me. I say "sort of" because there was never a "closed chapter" moment of transitioning from Gainesville to LA. I didn't even want to change my license plate for the longest time, because that would make it real and real was scary. But helping clients book acting jobs was like watching your boyfriend take another woman out every day.

When I started working with the agent, I worried that if I screwed up she was going to drop me as a client. But then we became very close, and the two of us ran the youth talent department together. As an agent, you are the liaison between finding talent and pitching them to casting directors and producers who can book them a job. If you represent kids who are minors, you also need to coordinate work permits, work hours, school hours, and Coogan Accounts. Child performers are required to have Coogan Accounts that save 15 percent of their gross earnings so no thievin' parents or unscrupulous folk can run away with the kids' money. *And yes*, you need to steer clear of parents living vicariously through their kids. The goal is to eventually usher these actors up into an adult division, or help them cultivate a career where they are not just actors selling fruit juice and laundry detergent.

The first Christmas after I got to LA, I saved up to go visit my family in Gainesville. The whole time I was there, I was worried about an audition I'd managed to get for

Hairspray on Broadway. Marissa Jaret Winokur was leaving the show and they needed a replacement. It seemed like a chance at my big break, and the audition was happening in LA as soon as I got back.

We were getting ready to go to Midnight Mass on Christmas Eve, and Morgana and I had been circling each other all day. She had been so bratty, and I think I was feeling my LA self. We have a tradition in our family in which everybody opens a present on Christmas Eve. Spoiler: it's always pajamas. We wear them to bed and to open presents in the morning.

I'd gotten my mom a beautiful suede jacket in LA. It was perfect to wear to Midnight Mass, so I wanted to give it to her early. This did not sit well with Miss Morgana.

"Well, why does Mom get an extra present?"

I lost my mind. "What are you talking about?" I yelled. "*Morgana.* Because she's our mom and she deserves a jacket to wear to church!"

"What's your problem?" she said.

"You're such an asshole," I said.

"Why are you such a fat bitch?"

That kind of thing wasn't going to hurt me anymore. "Yeah, you're right," I said. "I am."

This set her off and she lunged at me. As we fought, basically flailing our arms at each other, my mom began to yell, *"Take this shit outside!"*

We did, totally terrifying those neighbors, y'all. Brawlin'

at Christmas. My poor baby sister Abigail piped up. "I thought we were going to church."

Morgana went to swing on me like the front yard was the boxing ring.

"I have my audition for *Hairspray*!" I yelled. "DO NOT FUCK UP MY FACE!"

"I hate you."

I was literally about to go to jail for committing sistercide, I was that mad. My mom came out wearing her jacket, which did look awesome, thank you. "Get in the damn car so we can go to church. Jesus."

Happy birthday, Jesus. My mom drove, and I sat shotgun. The girls were in the back, with Morgana to my left. I could tell my mom was very upset.

"Hold hands!" she suddenly yelled.

I do what my mother tells me. I reached back, and Morgana took my hand. Then something magical happened. The thing we now talk about every Christmas. We both said at the exact same time, "I'm really sorry."

"Good," said my mom.

It was this authentic, genuine start to our new relationship. I went from thinking I could never even look at Morgana again to now talking to her four or five times a day. Just saying "Hey" from the car, or sending GIFs and voice memos. She's a great mom to her three kids. She's been married ten years. Looking back, I think we were playing roles. She was the diva and I was the selfless sister, and there was always a fight scene. I think it's worth going off-script with loved ones, maybe even acknowledging, "Hey, I know this is what we do, but can we just try something different?" For us, it was improvising to say, "I'm sorry." Trust me, that line was never in our scripts.

I did just okay at the *Hairspray* audition. I know now that I wasn't ready. It's funny that that had been all I was thinking about over Christmas, getting that job. I got a sister instead.

PRETTY SOON, MY AGENT AND I WERE THE HIGHEST-GROSSING DE-partment at that firm. And I enjoyed the work, because I got to go scout the talent at different showcases for my boss/ agent. This allowed me to sit in on acting classes and meet different actors. I eventually became an agent myself, and then I learned that it quickly becomes your life. It's basically a twenty-four-hour on-call job, because there is always an issue you must resolve or a breakdown to calm before the morning rush. The funny thing is, I learned so much about acting by being an agent. Some of my most important lessons in work came from those years, and I want to share them with you.

how to be an agent of change in your own life

Trust me, I am not up here on the mountaintop preaching a sermon about what you'd better do and not do. These are life tips that are still life goals for me as I work to live up to my potential. I've tripped, bluffed, fallen, and ah ha'd my way to understanding them. I just feel the need to pay it forward.

1. YOUR MIND IS A GARDEN AND YOUR THOUGHTS ARE THE SEEDS.

When I was a talent agent, we had families who remortgaged their homes just to give their kids the chance of acting. Talk about pressure, but they understood that you need to be in the place where it happens. For acting, that meant the two hubs—New York and Los Angeles.

If you want to nurture a passion, plant it where it has a chance to bloom. That's big-picture as far as location goes, but it's also about choosing a school or workplace that will allow you to grow. Ask yourself this simple question: Can I do what I want to be doing where I am now? We are so busy—being comfortable and afraid to try for fear of being uncomfortable.

When I wasn't making it as an actress, I told my mother that I thought I should just go home and go back to teaching preschool.

"You'll be miserable," my mother said.

"I'm miserable now, Mom."

"Then if you're going to be miserable either way," she said, "why not be miserable in LA doing what you love?"

She was right. I stayed in Los Angeles. Thanks, Mom.

2. BE YOUR OWN CLIENT.

Personally, I know I am better at sticking up for other people and negotiating on their behalf than I am doing so for myself. It's something I am still working on, so let's make a pact to do it together. It can be difficult to speak up for what you deserve, whether it's a promotion or a raise. So, make a case for yourself as if you were advocating for someone else. Don't talk about what you're entitled to, because that's about emotion. State facts. What is your value to the operation? If you are responsible for a company or project doing well, it's okay to say you deserve a little more of those dolla-dolla-bills, y'all.

3. DON'T BE A JERK-FACE.

I'm sorry, that wasn't an accusation. I know you're lovely. I just mean that when I was an agent, aggressive "shark"-like behavior was thought to be an asset. There is a kind, confident way to stand up for yourself, and I find that like attracts like. If you are kind, you will work with kind people. My clients were nice people who showed they were grateful to be doing work they loved. That's how you get more work. You can't keep anything you don't give away.

4. L'EGGO YOUR EGO.

Every once in a while, I would see a client resisting change. Finally, I would just have to say to the person, "Okay, these head shots aren't working. People aren't responding to them. Let's try another strategy."

Your ego will try to tell you that adapting is the same as failing. Growth comes in when you can be objectively constructive. What isn't working? What could be better? *Not* right or wrong. The universe is knocking at the door telling you that you need to change so you can have what you deserve, but your ego is the surly bouncer trying to ruin your night, confirming you're not on the list.

If you have been applying for positions or looking for investors but not getting them, take an ego-free, open look at your résumé or business plan. Maybe ask someone to look at it with you. Sometimes all we need is another perspective.

5. BIRDS OF A FEATHER EAT RAMEN TOGETHER.

When you're pursuing your dream, chances are you will be making sacrifices. Lots of them. Maintain a circle of friends who can cheer you on and let you crash on their couches if need be. When I couldn't afford acting classes, I read scripts with friends. We critiqued each other's work and got together to watch and discuss movies. We even paid for each other to get copies of head shots. It's not just about the lean times. You also want a support network when you achieve success. You need someone to check you—clothesline you—if you're getting too big for your britches or if you're working so hard you forget to enjoy the life you've created.

6. NO MUD, NO LOTUS.

When I was an agent scouting talent, I loved meeting people who had a spark, but one that wasn't fully cultivated. I was always signing actors who were unconventional, layered, and interesting. There are some agents who only want to represent the easy sell, which is annoying, but I digress . . . For me, I wanted to give the underdog a chance. We were good. I was on the team that represented Ariana Grande just as she was going on *Victorious* and also Dove Cameron from *Liv and Maddie* and *Descendants*. We represented Jordan Fisher of *Hamilton,* who brought home the Mirror Ball on *Dancing with the Stars,* and Hong Chau, who was nominated for a Golden Globe for *Downsizing* the very week I am writing this to you. And of course, Hannah Zeile, who plays fifteen-year-old me on *This Is Us.* (I didn't get her the job—she is so talented she didn't need me!)

Think about people you can mentor in your profession. I truly believe that you only get what you give. It's a lot of work to invest in people, but the rewards are huge. There's a loyalty and a beautiful bond that can't be broken when someone knows you took a chance on him or her. Believe me, I know.

7. READ THE FINE PRINT SERIOUSLY.

I had to cultivate that side of my brain, and I could do it because it was for other people. Now when I read contracts, I know what to look for and what to ask for. I feel empowered. When I get the feeling someone is trying to breeze over details to get me to a "yes," I simply say, "Before we go any further, I used to be an agent. You can't agent me."

"Oh," they say as they drop the façade. They stop pitching themselves or the company to me. When we're there on a level of mutual respect, we can just be real with each other. I can't stress enough how important it is to know what you're getting into, and not put yourself at a disadvantage by refusing to look at the fine print in your rush to be liked.

8. WHAT'S YOURS IS MEANT FOR YOU.

I have friends who originally thought they wanted to be actors but eventually chose to do other things. They just needed to be on a set to see what other dreams were available to them. They might have decided to become writers or producers, but if they never took the first step, they never would have known what their love really was.

I believe that everything happens as it should. What is yours is meant for you, and you can maintain it and there is an abundance for everyone. It's not always the journey we expect, but it's the one we need to take.

eight

WOO ME
WITH YOUR WORDS

Hey, you know what's not fun? Being strong-armed by your "friend" into creating an online dating profile. Especially in 2006. And especially when you thought you didn't need the interwebs to find a man. Or maybe you didn't even want a man.

But my friend told me about a plus-size dating website where she had a profile. First of all, I didn't even know those existed. Remember, this was 2006, so online dating was still a dirty secret. Telling your friends or family you met someone online was like confessing to joining a cult.

But my friend was insistent. Honestly, I should have known by how fast she raced to her computer all the time that something was up. I later learned she wanted me to sign up to see if the guys who were talking to her would try to hook up with me too. Okay, Carmen Sandiego, paranoid much? And so, I made my brief journey into the online world. Two weeks exactly.

Because that's how long it took for me to meet Marty. He lived in the north of England, and was the mayor of Babeville. Beautiful blue eyes and a real, genuine smile. Marty was a journalist and aspiring screenwriter, and a good one.

Once we exchanged emails and talked on the phone, I was doneskees. Put a fork in me, done. I told my mom and sisters right away. "Oh, okay," was the consensus. "Oh, cool." I don't think they took it seriously. When I told my friend I was going to remove my profile because I'd met a great guy, she freaked. And the interrogation began.

"He lives in England," she said.

"Yes," I said. "Sheffield."

"It doesn't matter where in England," she said, "because it's another country."

"Eventually Marty is going to come visit."

"Really?" she asked. "Has he seen all of you?" I knew exactly what she meant.

And yes, he had seen my size, curves, number on the scale, stomach, and still chose to write beautiful, poetic emails I woke up to every morning, without fail. I still have them printed in a binder that I would love to publish one day.

For seven months, we emailed, called, and sent letters,

cards, and pictures. I loved his voice and his accent. I fell truly, madly, deeply in like.

It wouldn't be real love, I promised myself, until he showed up.

And then he did. I went to pick him up at LAX and it was exactly like in the movies. I had been so nervous, and when I saw him, I thought, *There you are.* He was the One I had been wanting for so long. He and I were suddenly the only two people at baggage claim and time stood still. I am talking, like, the romantic movie scene you thought never actually happened.

He was supposed to come for two weeks, but he extended his ticket so many times. A month, then a month and a half, two months. We just clicked and had so much fun. It was his first time in America. He loved music, but especially hip-hop, so he had seen all the pictures, movies, and documentaries about it. But to be in California, the land of Tupac and Snoop, was amazing for him. Also, he was from this coal-mining town in the north of England, and now suddenly there's all this sun. I got to experience so many LA firsts again. We went to the beach and San Diego, and I introduced him to Mexican food.

When he left, it was an emotional goodbye, to put it lightly. I was sobbing on the way back to my car, crying so much that an airport employee with a kind face quietly said to me, "Don't worry, he's gonna come back." How did he know who or what I was crying about? It was just what

I needed to hear. Marty's plane hadn't even taken off and I already missed him desperately. It's funny how people talk you out of happiness. "You need to go to England, Chrissy," a friend said. I agreed, but then, she added why: "Make sure he doesn't have a wife and a bunch of little Martys."

I knew he didn't. We went on like this for almost a year, with him always coming to me in LA. We had no money, but it didn't matter. We clicked creatively and we loved each other. We took that day trip to Montecito—the one where I, you know, manifested knowing Oprah—and visited Butterfly Beach, right by the Four Seasons Biltmore. It was like an ad for your dream California vacay. We took the 101 to this beautiful place, palm trees lining the beach. It is a hidden gem, with no more than a handful of people walking the sand as the tide rose. "We'll come back here," he said.

We did. We went back a few months later after we had dated just over a year. We parked the car on the shoulder of the road just as the sun was setting, so we rushed down to watch it. He ran just a little bit ahead of me.

"Okay, hold on," I said.

He turned around fast, and was suddenly down on one knee.

"Chrissy, will you do me the honor of being my wife?"

Did I say something poetic and beautiful? Something along the lines of "Yes, I want to go through this life's journey with you at my side. I want us to be together as we grow into the people we want to be."

No, I just started yelling.

"Wait, wait, wha—whaaat?" I stammered. "Are you serious? Like seriously serious?"

He looked confused, so I managed to sputter out, "Yes. Yes, of course!"

We had talked about getting married. It just seemed natural, since we had never felt this way about another person. But I never expected that he had saved money to get me a ring, or that it would be so soon. Back then, I would never presume someone would be working in secret to do something to make me happy.

After the hyperventilating subsided, I made the first call to the person I knew would understand my happiness.

"Grams," I said. "Marty just proposed—we're engaged!"

"Congratulations, my darlin'!" Grams said.

"I'm so happy," I said.

"Oh honey, that's what matters. And I am so happy for you."

My family was so excited, and my grandma wanted to plan the wedding with my sister Monica. They envisioned us all gathering in Florida. But we couldn't afford to fly out, and they couldn't afford to pay to bring us there. No one in my family had even *met* Marty because we couldn't afford to visit Gainesville.

I told them I would just have a simple January wedding in Santa Barbara on Butterfly Beach. Just us, the officiant, a photographer, and the tide as it rose. I think they were really crushed when I told them we couldn't afford to come to Florida for a wedding, no matter how small they pictured it. So, I reached out to Mark, my biological father.

I had his email address. "Hey, I just wanted to let you know that I am engaged. He's a great guy; we're going to get married." I paused at the keyboard, then swallowed my pride and continued typing.

"I don't know if there's any help you might be willing to give us or anything you would like to talk about."

I pressed SEND before I could second-guess myself. I pictured him reading the message and being happy for me. I assumed he'd write back, "Chrissy, I am not in a financial position to give you money, but I wish you the best." That alone would have meant something.

He never replied.

I didn't anticipate how lonely I would feel planning the wedding for just the two of us. Just me and Mr. Wilson, stranded on Gilligan's Cryland. My sister Monica would send me pictures of wedding dresses with the Subject Line "CUTE! Maybe?" I loved the dresses, of course, but I wanted her to be there. I wanted to have a shower and all the things a girl wants to share with her sisters, grandmother, and mother. Crying and laughing while we made couture wedding dresses out of toilet paper. I wanted a cake and paper bells and fancy napkins. Yes, well, she's getting *married*. *Let's all celebrate!*

Saturday, January 5, our wedding day, we woke up in the Montecito Inn to a torrential downpour. The *Los Angeles Times* headline was "Storm Now Has Its Eye on the Southland." A thousand homes in Orange County were being evacuated, and a million people had already lost power. There were four inches of rain and hurricane-force winds. And an outdoor wedding.

We moved it to the Santa Barbara courthouse, which is honestly beautiful if any of you ladies or gentlemen are getting married there; it just was not what my heart was set on. It was freezing that day, and I had a short wedding dress. When I left the hotel to get my makeup done, I stepped off the curb and my sandal slipped off. There it went, floating away with a river of rainwater down the storm drain. I had to go back to my room for another pair of shoes. All the things that girls dream their wedding will be seemed to float away with that sandal.

That was okay, I told myself, because honestly Marty and I loved each other deeply and as long as we were together, that was all that mattered. Okay? Okay.

We raced into the courthouse, and as we were dripping and freezing, the clerk gave us a pitying look.

"Congratulations," she said. "Just so you know, when it rains on your wedding day, it's good luck."

"What about a deluge?" I said. "What about a tropical storm? What does *that* mean?"

The ceremony took only a few minutes. We had dinner at a restaurant next to the hotel and spent the night at the Montecito Inn. That would be our honeymoon. I wish we could have done a real honeymoon, but when you're struggling financially, you're not going to have that. We had each other, and that was enough.

And we had food. Marty was a big guy, and he had gained weight right before we met. We enjoyed each other's company, and we gained the weight that many couples gain when they are just happy together. But I wasn't aware of how much weight I had gained, and soon I had put on thirty pounds.

I was working sixty hours a week as an agent while he worked part-time so he could pursue his dream to be a screenwriter. I paid the majority of the bills, so I put my dreams on the back burner. It was easier to say my acting career was never going to happen than to try and fail miserably. Marty also made it clear that he didn't really vibe with the personalities of performers, which were basically all the people in my circle of friends. It's not that my friends were always "on," but they were funny and their comedy was broad and bold. He felt we were all trying to one-up each other getting some bigger laugh.

His distaste for performers was awkward, because being one was still my dream in my heart of hearts. I was averaging two auditions a year, and in 2009 I landed a role on an episode of *My Name Is Earl*, playing a cheerleader named . . . guess . . . Chunk. So I spent a *chunk* of the money on a trip to Florida. My family and I split the cost of a condo for a week of vacay so they could finally meet my husband.

And they did not get along.

Look, nobody got crazy or anything. It's just that Marty is quiet and reserved, and my family is the opposite of quiet and reserved. You have to fight to get a word in edgewise, and they expect you to keep up. They liked him, but when he didn't say much, they weren't sure that he liked them. It just never clicked. He felt crappy; they felt crappy. Me too. I felt both sides were being judged, and I was so protective of them both.

A highlight of the trip was going to visit my Grams and being able to say, "This is my husband, Marty." We spent two nights with her, and it was so wonderful. All she wanted for me was to be happy, and Marty responded to that. He thought she was lovely and kind.

Back in LA after that vacation, I learned an important lesson about marriage.

the shrouded supreme

For the first two years of my relationship with Marty, we ordered a lot of pizza. I worked a lot, and who doesn't enjoy two of the greatest man-made inventions: pizza and delivery?

"I'll have the Supreme," he would say every single time.

And inside, I would think each and every time, *Oh God, that comes with bell pepper.* I like olives and onions, but I don't do the bell pepper.

But I would say to myself, *Chrissy, marriage is about compromise.* If he liked them, I could pick them off. No bigs.

One day, a ridiculously long time into our Pizza Supreme–eating relationship, I noticed he knocked a couple of bell peppers off. I mean, who *was* this man?

"Do you like bell peppers?"

"No," he said, almost guiltily.

"What?"

"I order them for you."

"I order them for *you*."

It took *years* for us to realize that. For *years* we were treating each other with such kid gloves that we were afraid to say, "Hey babe, I don't like the bell peppers." Or communicate effectively by asking, "Can you make your half Supreme and I'll just have olives?" It was a lovely sacrifice because we did care about each other so deeply, but at our own expense.

I think you have to peek-a-boo look at your pepper-roos. The things you put up with in romantic relationships and friendships. It's okay to say, "This isn't working for me" or "I don't like this." Because your friends and significant others probably want you to be happy, right? (Unless they're sociopaths, in which case, R to the U to the N.)

Whatever your bell pepper is, if you are doing something or putting up with something because you love someone, consider checking in with that person to make sure that is really love in action to him or her. Because *you* are not the authority on what makes others feel loved. They are. Ask them.

nine

LOST ANGELES

You know that terrible moment when you realize your car won't start? The ignition just won't turn. You are certain that if you give it a second the car will change its mind. But it doesn't. Welcome to the summer of 2007, when my trusty Ford Focus was trying to tell me it was tired. It had gotten me to LA and carried me through my first two years there, but it had decided the parking garage of the agency where I was a junior agent would be a good place to die.

The funny thing is, the lights still worked, and the radio. My car was a lot like my life at the time. The lights were on, the music was playing, but something wasn't clicking enough to get the car moving.

I had to get it towed, but I wasn't ready to say goodbye. The problem was that I barely had enough money to pay for the tow truck, let alone get a new car. It was the ignition switch, and I discovered, just from desperation, that if I shimmied the key in the ignition just so, I could still get it started. The magic number was fourteen times. I wasn't giving up on acting, or Los Angeles, and I wasn't giving up on this car.

God, I was trying. I worked every day until 7 p.m., and then raced over to my second job at CVS, where I worked as a cashier until midnight. One time at that job, my manager came up to me.

"You do your makeup so nicely; do you want to work in the Beauty department?"

"Wellll," I said, "if I have to work solely on commission, no. That gives me anxiety." I just didn't want to have to try to up-sell anybody to make more money.

"No, no," she said. "We'd pay you more."

Sold.

So, I was in the Beauty department at CVS when this supernice man, Michael Levin, came in looking for something. I always liked when customers asked me for help because it was as if we were on a hunt for something together. We got to talking—as you can guess, I got to talking with all my customers—and I told him I was an actress but I worked at an agency.

"Why don't you come to the TV Land awards?"

"What do you mean?"

"I produce the show," he said. I confess I didn't know what the heck that meant at that point.

"Oh, okay."

"It's in an airplane hangar in the Santa Monica airport. Sally Field is gonna do a bit about the Flying Nun."

"Oh. I love Sally Field," I said. "I really, really love her."

So, I and my life-support car went to the TV Land awards. I brought my friend Julia, who was another client of my manager. My manager was going back and forth between Florida and LA, bringing in new waves of talent. As we pulled up to the show, Julia was still changing her clothes in the car because she'd just gotten off her waitressing shift. The moment I started wondering if we'd dressed fancy enough, we got in the valet line right behind Morgan freaking Freeman.

All his movies flashed before my eyes. *Shawshank, Se7en, Driving Miss Daisy* . . . Julia and I got out and I was just beyond to be sharing this time and space with an acting legend. Mr. Morgan Freeman, because I can't just call him Morgan, was walking right in front of us when the valet started yelling for me.

"Miss, miss!" he said. "Your car won't start."

I turned. Mr. Morgan Freeman turned. The whole world turned as my car held up the arrivals at an awards show.

"Just shimmy it!" I yelled back. "You gotta try fourteen times!" I mimed it for him. "Just go like 'boom, boom, boom.'"

"What do you mean?"

"Just try it."

It worked! I tell ya, you gotta do what you gotta do.

I WAS SHIMMYING THE IGNITION OF MY OWN LIFE, TRYING TO GET IT moving. My next attempt to break through was auditioning for *American Idol* that July. My friend Dakota was another client of my manager, and was really one of the most talented singers I had ever heard. I always tried to encourage and support her, but I don't think she quite believed in herself at that point. We were talking about auditioning together, but she decided it just wasn't for her. I wasn't going to give up so easily. And besides, what did I have to lose?

The closest audition was in San Diego, at Qualcomm Stadium, which was then home to the San Diego Chargers. Marty and I drove all the way down there, waiting in line forever because there were twelve thousand people trying out. They had us all sit as though we were watching a football game, doing sing-alongs to songs like—what else?— "California Dreamin'." We were there for eight hours, with the sun beating down on us the whole time. They had cameramen walking around and eventually, one walked over to me.

"What can you tell us about the day?" he asked. "Two words."

"Two things I'm gonna tell you," I said. "Sun. Screen." Yes, I know that's one word, but I could barely think. I was wearing a jean skirt and was getting third-degree burns on my shins.

My number was finally called, and I made my way down

to the field. They had about twenty tents set up, with two to three judges per tent. The handlers lined up the folks who were auditioning in rows of five, and you had literally thirty seconds to sing whatever you had prepared.

I decided to sing "Heavy" from *Dreamgirls*, because I thought it was appropriate, but also fun and different. I was in the middle with two people on either side of me. The girl right before me sang "Cruisin'" and did a great job.

I sang my bit and the guy, who I could tell was the lead judge, just said, "Okay." The next two people sang, and then we waited to find out if one of us was going to get that coveted yellow piece of paper that meant we'd advance to the next round.

"You know," the guy started, stretching it out. "This year we're really taking it to the next level . . ."

There are some people you just know are making up stuff to say. Stringing words together that amount to nothing. This was that guy. "And I just don't know if you guys have the next level of talent that we need."

"I think you're wrong," I said. Everybody looked at me like I had grown a second head. One of the girls blurted out, "Welp."

"Excuse me?" said the guy.

"I just think you're wrong," I repeated. "I think you're making a terrible choice." I owned it. In that moment, I stood up for myself.

There were two female judges in the tent right next

to ours. The guy's "Excuse me" had echoed so loudly that they turned to watch our little show. One of the women, a blonde, looked right at me. "Come here," she said. "Come here."

I marched over to their tent, not sure if this woman just wanted to "put me in my place" or what.

"Sing for me," she said. "Audition for me. If he said no, audition for me."

There were two people left in her group of five waiting to sing. I turned to them and said, "Sorry for cutting." And I thought. *Okay, here goes.* And I began to sing my heart out.

"Heavvvvvvvy."

"Um," she said, when I was done. She gave the guy judge a "What are you thinking?" look, and she gave me that yellow piece of paper.

"Thank you," I said. I looked back and up to where Marty was sitting and waved my little yellow ticket at him. He jumped up screaming and ran down the bleachers to get closer to me. He had been right there, sitting in that sun with me and for me. I was—and remain—so grateful for his support.

I was one of about 250 people picked that day. The officials took me back to the corral, where they took all my information and acted like I'd signed my life away. Like this was the Hunger Games or something. This was just at the dawn of social media, and they told us if we had any social handles, we had to delete them immediately. Can you imagine?

About three weeks later, there were the second-round auditions at a hotel back in Los Angeles. We were in the banquet halls and the place was completely mobbed. I was feeling good, so excited. Then I started to look around. Why was that girl in a bikini? Why was that guy dressed like a clown? There were people here who were just trying to get on TV.

They asked me to learn a song, Gwen Stefani's "The Sweet Escape," to do on camera before I went in for my actual audition. There is a tricky rap-sing part in that tune, but that worked in my favor 'cause your girl here loves some hip-hop. I wondered whether they were seeing if I could pull it off or trying to embarrass me. Probably a little bit of both.

Once that was done, I went for the real audition. It was held in a massive room, packed with thirty crew members. There were tons of lights and tons of cameras. "Oh," I said. "Oh dear."

The judges were two executive producers of *American Idol*: Nigel Lythgoe and Simon Fuller.

"So, you're a talent agent," said Simon, the British clip of his voice sounding so much like Simon Cowell's. They even looked alike.

"Yeah!"

"Then you must know what talent is," said Nigel, who is also English.

"Yes, I do."

I told them I was going to sing "Heavy" and they nodded. "Good choice," said Simon. But I was about five seconds into it when Nigel started yelling, "Hold on, hold on!"

I froze, and he said, "Why are you stomping your foot?"

I didn't think I was. "I was just getting into it."

"I thought you were supposed to know what talent is," Nigel sniffed. I knew what he was doing. I had watched the show enough to know that they were degrading me to try to get a rise out of me. The cameras were rolling and fiery contestants or down-in-flames auditions make good television.

"Hmm, yeah, I don't know that I like the sound of your voice," said Simon.

I nodded. He was entitled to his opinion.

"I don't think you know how to use it yet," said Nigel.

"Oh, okay," I said.

"That's it?" said Simon.

"Okay?" parroted Nigel.

"If you don't think I'm ready or right, then thank you for this opportunity," I said.

I started to walk away and they were sputtering, as if they couldn't believe I was folding so easily.

"Thank you so much for your time," I said. I walked out the door and of course the camera was right in my face. There was a host there, who I should add was no Ryan Seacrest, and he asked me, "Do you think they made a bad decision?"

"It's their decision and a matter of opinion," I said. "But I'm glad I had the experience." I started to walk away, and they followed me. I turned around. "For the record, guys," I said, "I'm not going to give you any good television, so you don't have to follow me anymore."

The cameraman turned around on a dime.

I had learned a lesson. I advocated for myself at Qualcomm Stadium, because I really, really wanted that opportunity. But once I had a better sense of what the process was all about, I realized it wasn't something I wanted to fight for. *American Idol* wasn't the dream for me. I don't want anyone thinking I'm a hater. I feel those shows have the power to help an artist become him- or herself, but looking back, I am at peace with not getting on the show.

AFTER YEARS OF THE FOURTEEN-SHIMMY METHOD, MY FORD FOCUS met its final resting place in a car accident on Wilshire Boulevard. A guy who was late for an interview at a talent management company—so LA, I know—came across the entire road and hit me on the passenger side. I was so scared, because I was about an inch away from being seriously injured. Life, as John Lennon said, is what happens to you when you are busy making other plans.

He was a kid, and did everything he could to try to get out of reporting the accident to the police and his insurance company. I called Marty from the side of the road and he came and met me.

"That stupid kid was on his way to be some stupid assistant for some stupid management company," I said. "He can't even watch where the hell he's going."

There was such violence in my voice that Marty looked at me like I was crazy.

I took a deep breath. "I'm just angry and scared," I said. "This poor kid was trying to get to an interview and is running late, so he was driving irresponsibly. He made a mistake."

Years later, I ended up with a manager who worked at the office where the kid was going for an interview. I would always look for him. I honestly hope he got the job.

Michael Levin and I would meet again, years after our first encounter. In December 2017, I was back at the Barker airplane hangar in Santa Monica, this time for the Critics' Choice Awards. *This Is Us* was up for two awards, and the whole cast was there all dressed up. I was so excited. We were on the red carpet when I suddenly heard someone yell my name. It was Michael!

"What are you here for?" I asked. I was thrilled to see him again.

"I'm producing the awards," he said. "Chrissy. Do you believe all this? You were at *CVS*."

"I know!"

Believe me, I know. I was in a CVS parking lot at midnight, praying my car would start so I could get home and sleep before getting up at 7 a.m. to start my other workday. You just never know when it's going to click for you. If you're having hard times right now, whatever shimmy trick you have to do to keep going, take a mental picture. I want you to look back on this part of your life and thank yourself for not giving up.

ten

IF NOTHING CHANGES, NOTHING CHANGES

I don't blame Sly, I swear.

It was a Friday in September, the night before my thirtieth birthday party. Marty and I went to the ArcLight movie theater in LA to see Sylvester Stallone in *The Expendables*. There are about a million gunshots in the movie, and I am not sure if it was the sound or the darkness. But suddenly, I began to have heart palpitations. Like I was about to die.

"Babe, something's wrong," I whispered to Marty. "My heart is beating out of my chest."

He helped me out of the dark of the theater, and I sat on a bench in the lobby. My heart was still racing, and I just felt out of control, barely able to breathe. People were staring at me. I must have looked awful, because Marty looked *scared*.

"I'm calling an ambulance," he said.

He dialed 911 and they came right away with a stretcher.

The EMTs were three incredibly nice men, but I felt so vulnerable and embarrassed. They put the stretcher on the ground and asked me to lie down on it. *What if they can't lift me?* I thought. *What if I'm too heavy?*

They took me away in the ambulance, with Marty holding my hand on the way to the nearest hospital. I was admitted immediately and had an EKG and all these other tests with abbreviations I didn't understand. Words were thrown at me that I just nodded at. A young physician came into my room. "Well, you didn't have a heart attack," he said. "There's also no sign of stroke."

"Oh, okay," I said, relieved but bewildered.

"We're going to do a stress test and the whole gamut to make sure everything is fine. You have really good numbers; there's nothing wrong with your triglycerides and your cholesterol is fine."

"Okay," I said.

"But you'll want to lose weight."

"Yeah."

The attending doctor came in, shaking her head. The first thing she said was, "You know, if you were my daughter, I would force you to get a gastric bypass."

She was my age, and she talked to me like I was a child.

"Seriously," she said.

"Okay, thanks," I said, thinking, *Awesome. Thanks for your bedside manner. Thank you for your unsolicited opinion.*

She wanted me to stay there for observation, so Marty

canceled the birthday party he had planned. My friends and I were going to have dinner at a restaurant, then do cake and presents afterward at my house. We let everyone know it was canceled and I called my family.

I stayed two nights and most of Sunday. The Saturday doctor came into my room, and I could immediately tell she was kinder than Dr. Boorish-Bypass. I smoothed the sheets as if I were hosting a guest.

"We did a whole workup," she said. "Everything is fine. Do you have a history of panic attacks or anxiety?"

"No!" I said, like there was something wrong with that.

"Well, it appears you had a severe anxiety attack."

"Hmm," I said. I had no idea anxiety could feel like dying.

"Chrissy," she said, leaning in. "Is there past trauma that you haven't dealt with?"

"What are you talking about?!" I said, feigning shock. I was so delusional, so clueless about my own life and body. "No."

That night in the hospital I thought about what the doctor had said. Anxiety is one of the worst things you can experience in your whole life. The more you resist, the more it persists. I learned pretty quickly that I had to lean in to my anxiety. And accept it. Or try to. I had a much-needed conversation with myself.

"What's the worst thing in the world that could happen?" I asked myself aloud.

"I could die," I answered.

"Okay."

"You're right," I conceded. "That's not the end of the world."

It's just not. I don't believe death is forever. I had to surrender control. Whatever happens, happens. The thing is, I could die, but I just didn't want to.

Let's say it was a process. When I got out of the hospital, I worried that something was really wrong with me physically and they didn't catch it. They had prescribed Xanax, but, honestly, I think I only ever took half a pill. I didn't want any part of it. There were some nights when I would cry myself to sleep, with poor Marty just having to watch me, unable to comfort me. I felt like such a failure that he had seen me that way. And he felt like a failure because he couldn't help me.

I was scared. And the only thing that I could really do was try to lose weight. I was definitely my heaviest weight ever during this time. I made it a point to thank God that nothing was wrong and I had the ability to change it. I went on a 2,000-calorie diet, and Marty and I walked every night for twenty minutes. No gastric bypass. Nothing extreme.

In four months, I lost ninety pounds and I felt great. Marty was helpful on the diet and never tried to sabotage me. But then, losing weight got hard again. I told a friend I couldn't do it on my own anymore. I was falling back into old patterns. She told me I should start going to a support group.

I found one that was held in a place I passed by every morning, but honestly, it was like I magically arrived right where I needed to be. I was just suddenly walking through the door. It was in a square room with a circle of chairs. I had an orange bucket bag from Michael Kors, and I put it down on the seat next to me with a sigh. *Oh God*, I thought. *It's come to this.*

I stayed completely quiet at my first group meeting, just listening, but what I heard really resonated. Once you stop making everything about yourself and your feelings, things just kind of click. You're forced to be honest with what's going on with you, deep down, and what you're doing to yourself.

People told stories, and it was like they were describing my life. I heard stories about things that I thought only I did and felt shameful for—like not being able to wait for the food to be cooked in the microwave and eating the burrito that is still half-frozen. Or throwing food away in the trash can in your house but contemplating digging it out because it is on top and hasn't touched anything else . . . I've done that too.

You go out to lunch, but all you can think about is what you are having for dinner. The next meal. I really did think that I was the only person who thought that way. This wasn't about the joy of food, but the need to fill the void and eat our emotions.

Most of the people were hilarious, wonderful, smart people. *Oh, we've almost got it together*, I thought, looking around. We have these successful lives and relationships, but there's this huge component that's not locking in yet. Then there were those of us who were just a mess, and simply couldn't function. I never thought I was better than another person because I didn't eat a whole loaf of bread at one time. Not to say I couldn't; I just haven't.

I sympathized with those folks so deeply. It doesn't matter how addiction manifests. Addiction is addiction is addiction. Whether you're a drug addict or a food addict, it's the same thing. It's just that food is easily accessible and acceptable, and you have to consume it in order to survive.

That was really . . . *oof*, it was hard for me to realize I had such an obsession with food that the feeling it gave me was an addiction.

I kept going back. My third week, a gentleman sidled up to me during the coffee break.

"I noticed you last week," he said with a slight Brooklyn accent. "And then I noticed your really great purse."

"Thank you," I said, unconsciously putting my hand to push back my hair—and showing my wedding ring.

"I'm gay," he stage-whispered.

He was so funny, and I loved that he had a little edge to him. He was definitely a man who spoke his mind, which of course I admired. Before too long, I learned he was also an actor.

We became very close friends, and I started to look forward to seeing him at the support group because I didn't feel alone.

Initially, I went once a week. But I became obsessive. Once a week, then twice, then three times, and then I found a meeting to go to every morning. I could tell Marty resented how much attending group was taking over my life. *Our* life.

"I don't see why you can spend an hour in a support group and not in the gym," he said a couple of times. I felt my food obsession was a symptom, not the issue. And I knew I needed to fix the mental stuff before I could hope to have a lasting relationship with my body.

I became a mirror to Marty, forcing him to examine his own stuff. He began to exercise more. And when we put the food down, we realized we just didn't have much in common. The more we started focusing on ourselves as individuals, the more the wedge between us grew. He never wanted to do yoga with me and I never wanted to hike with him. Even though it's okay for couples to not always be together, it felt like we were actively choosing to spend time apart and using our schedules as an excuse for what was really happening.

It was scary to realize this. In a perfect world, we would have had time to talk and work on our relationship, but I was working so hard, usually about seventy to eighty hours a week. When you're an agent you have to make yourself 100 percent available to your clients, because you never know what's gonna happen. I got home so late that by the time I had a minute to take a breath, it was time to go to work again. With a group meeting first, mind you.

There was such a feeling of camaraderie. I was probably a month in when a guy came over and told me about a retreat being held at a campground near Palm Springs and he said he could get me a free ticket. *Um, yes.*

It really was like a camp, where you shared bunk beds and everything. The retreat was led by Cherie Meagher, who was thin and blond and put together, such a cute little thing. "Don't let this fool you," she said. "I used to weigh nearly three hundred pounds. Now I dye my hair, use spray tan, and put makeup on." She was so open about her vulnerabilities that it set the tone for the weekend. "None of us are perfect," she said. I soaked it all up like a sponge.

One of our activities at camp was called "Drop the Rock." For this, we were led into the middle of the forest to find a rock. Everything that you want to let go of, you allow to flow into that rock. Then, when you drop it—or throw it—all the feelings and emotions that are holding you back stay in that forest. We also had to write a letter to our future selves, with the understanding that Cherie would mail them to us exactly one year later.

"You're special just for being alive," I wrote. "You've got this. You can do this. Take it one day at a time. Take it one *hour* at a time." I told myself to remember all that I had come through so far in my life. I had overcome five elementary schools, my parents' divorce, the abuse of my stepfather, and no longer being the baby, and I'd managed to scrape a life together on my own two feet in Hollywood. "You are capable of having the life you deserve." All of us believe that, even if with only .1 percent of our beings. Or 5 or 10 percent. But there is some part of us that tells us we deserve to have happiness. Because we all want to get off the ride when it's not fun anymore.

We handwrote those letters, and of course I decorated the heck out of the letter and envelope with drawings and stickers. *As one does.*

Getting away from the everyday on that retreat gave me the time and space I desperately needed to focus on reality. It was the fat camp I'd always wanted to attend. Who doesn't want to go someplace where they can be with a lot of people dealing with the same thing? It was heaven. On the way home, I was thinking about how lovely it was that this guy offered me a ticket. He didn't even know me. *Oh*, I thought, *that's the universe. I'm supposed to be doing this.*

ABOUT TWO MONTHS IN, I WAS CLOCKING DAILY MEETINGS AND still hadn't spoken when my friend suggested that I start.

"Maybe there's something you want to talk about," he said.

"Oh, I don't know . . ." I replied. Translation: Nope, I'm good.

He knew I was scared, so he put on his fake lecture tone. "There is something really powerful about getting it off your chest in a group setting," he said. "Maybe others have gone through the same, and perhaps they can give you some good advice."

"Okay, alright. Alright, alright."

It's funny because in "real life," I hold court and I tell stories for days. I'm an actress. And in the room, I was all, "Please don't pay attention to me. I don't wanna talk about it. This is too hard."

But I decided it wasn't about me. Hearing a new person's story helps those farther along remember their early days when they couldn't stop eating and didn't know why.

Now I just had to talk. There were plenty of people dying to get things off their chests that day, so I let them go first. Meanwhile, my friend was across the room alternating between giving me encouraging "okay, now you" smiles and shooting daggers. Finally, I started to talk, and I honestly don't remember what I said that first time. I'm sure it had to do with work and how miserable I was. I was continually asked to do more and more work, but I didn't have any support.

It was hard finding a balance between work and marriage. There are women who work incredible hours and then come home and cook and nurture their families. I wasn't one of those women. I think that became an issue with Marty too. It's not that Marty had been coddled, but his mother took care of him and his dad. Maybe as a man he wanted to be taken care of. But the fact is that he worked four or five hours a day. My feeling was, if I am doing all this to support your writing, you shouldn't have a problem cooking dinner or doing a load of laundry. On top of that, I couldn't help having resentment about our financial situation. I was working so hard but had nothing to show for it.

Being tired all the time made all these issues easy to brush aside.

When I thought about all my frustrations, I reminded myself what a supportive person my husband was. We truly loved each other, and very deeply. He tried to help me do music on the weekends, just because I needed a creative outlet. He had done music engineering in the UK, and he could help me write lyrics. He would mix different pieces of music together, getting samples from old school songs, and we would try to collaborate. We had fun, but it can be hard to be creative with your significant other because if you can't even discuss pizza toppings, you may be afraid to tell him you don't like something he's added to the song you're working on. There was that. But we still had a lot of fun and I was grateful.

Marty never said anything about the support group meetings, but the longer I did them, the clearer it was that he didn't like them. I was putting myself first and figuring out the true nature of my relationship with food in the past, and moving forward, I didn't notice how neglected Marty was feeling.

He started to exercise even more, and Marty lost enough weight that his wedding ring no longer fit. Whenever I mentioned getting it resized, he told me he'd get around to it. He mainly exercised by taking hikes near our apartment during the day. He hiked in the afternoon, after working mornings at a small PR firm.

Because I didn't hike with him, he ended up finding someone in his office to hike with. Betty.

I admit I was not initially fond of Betty. Marty had talked about this woman at work who was cool, but I didn't think much of it. She was married and she had kids. But one night Marty and I were walking around the Galleria mall when this woman suddenly yelled in our direction.

"Martini!"

It was Betty. With her husband. Martini was her pet name for Marty. *Hold on*, I thought. *Hold on. This grown-ass woman with a husband and children just called my husband by a nickname. Who is this bitch?*

Later Marty assured me there was nothing to worry about, and proceeded to tell me all this personal stuff that she had confided in him. Medical things and personal information that you might not want to tell your own husband. Much less *my* husband. Hmph. Okay, but hmph.

One day I left work early because I had an audition.

There is about one decent role for a plus-size woman a year, which meant this was my yearly audition. I went home first, to change my shirt and pick up my head shot. Driving up, I saw Marty pulling into the garage. I remember my exact thought was, *Oh cool. He's going to go hike, but I'll still get to say hello to him.*

Then a car that was parked out front just peeled away, going way faster than you would expect in our little residential area. It was Betty's car.

That was weird, I thought. I didn't think it was suspicious; it was just weird.

"Was that Betty?" I asked when I went in.

"Yeah, we were gonna go hiking," he said, sitting on the couch.

"Why did she speed away?"

"I don't know?" He said it like a question. He's not a liar. He's not an actor. He really didn't know.

"Does *she* feel guilty that she is hiking with you?" I asked. "That she didn't expect me to be here?"

"Well, we were gonna smoke together."

"Smoke weed," I said. "And then, like, hike?"

"Yeah."

If I smoked up I couldn't even walk, much less hike. But then I thought, *Why is another woman in my house without me? And the two of you are getting high together?* Okay. Okay.

"You have to understand this is a weird relationship," I said. "She calls you Martini, you guys go hiking together,

167

you know her *personal* information. Let's put the shoe on the other foot. What if there was some guy at work who called me some nickname like Chrissmas . . ."

"Chrissmas?"

"Let's say Chrissmas," I said. "And we went hiking together and we spent all this time together . . ."

"Oh yeah," he said slowly. "That would bother me."

"Uh-huh," I said. "So, what the hell?"

"I get it. That was not my goal."

"I mean, I know you weren't going to smoke out on the damn trail; I get it if you're gonna do that, you do it here. But it doesn't make me feel good."

I felt guilty for being mad at him. I knew in my heart Marty was such a good man that he would never, ever cheat on me. I didn't think he was even having an *emotional* affair, but I just kept replaying the vision of her racing off. She was in my house while I was at work. And I wouldn't even have known about it if I didn't have an audition.

And no, I didn't get the job.

The guilt didn't leave me. I was trying so hard to get ahold of my relationship with my body and break my habit of eating my emotions and of equating food with sharing love. I didn't know how to spend time with Marty without using.

MY FRIEND ENDED UP LEAVING THE PROGRAM. HE WASN'T DOING well, and we lost touch. I got close to another person who I love, but then *she* stopped coming to group, too. *Huh, what does it all mean,* I asked myself, *if people keep leaving?* Seeing that made me question everything. I was losing weight, but was I getting addicted to going to group? And if my friends eventually gave up, what would stop *me from doing the same?*

A thin woman approached me after a group session ended and asked if I wanted to partner with her. Our agreement was that I would email her what I was planning to eat for breakfast, lunch, dinner, and snack. Then I would give her a report in the evening about how things had gone. It was going well, but she was a little tougher than I'd hoped.

We did this for three months when she said something that did me in.

"You know, Chrissy . . ." she said. "We all know that you're in pain by the way that you dress." She thought I dressed inappropriately for my size and that my clothes were too tight. "I know you focus on your face, because I did the same thing. You don't want anyone to look at your body."

Dayum. I was so confused by what she had said that I talked to a couple of people in the group. One told me: "Just because she's kept the weight off doesn't mean she's done with her issues. Because we're all dealing with this stuff."

This was a time when I was trying to feel comfortable in my body no matter what I was wearing. Maybe it made her uncomfortable to see me feeling so comfortable. Did she think that fat was such a bad thing that she couldn't accept it on anybody? That I was supposed to hide?

I couldn't get past it, and her words hurt me so much that I was discouraged from continuing in the group. I stopped going and decided I had learned enough to go it alone. But deep down, I knew I was making an excuse so that I didn't have to go back and face her.

Slowly, Marty and I fell back into old habits. I managed to keep the weight off for a while, but then the pounds started to come back. More important than any number was the fact that I had returned to my old crutch of numbing myself with food. It started with having a little bit more here and there, but it's a slippery slope. One night I treated myself to a cheeseburger and fries. That became a weekly thing, and then more often. I would get busy and decide the best use of my time would be to just run through the drive-thru. Or I would have salty food and say, "Well, now I need sweet." Sometimes you don't realize you're eating the feelings you can't handle.

One day I came home to find the letter I had written myself. Cherie had kept her promise to mail it a year later to the day. It was trippy to see that letter arrive in the mail. I'd completely forgotten about it.

I opened it right away. "You are capable of having the life you deserve," I read. I was glad that I had lost the weight and kept it off for a while, but I knew I was slipping. *Is this ever going to change?* I asked myself. When they scare you with statistics such as 95 percent of people who lose weight gain it back, it is easy to feel hopeless. And I did. I decided I'd made a mistake leaving the program. That was on the long list of mistakes I began to create. I was so excited to receive the letter, but it opened a Pandora's box of guilt and blame. I had to get comfortable with being uncomfortable again. I needed to recommit, if not to finding another support group, to at least putting my health and myself first.

MARTY'S PARENTS CAME TO VISIT EVERY SUMMER FOR A MONTH. IT always coincided with June Gloom, the time when LA has cloudy, overcast skies and cooler temperatures. His parents would sleep on our pull-out couch, and I would play tour guide. Marty or I would drive them everywhere, and I would plan excursions, such as a trip to Las Vegas one year and Santa Barbara the next.

This year they were set to arrive on a day that I had a long-scheduled lunch with a friend. And I was going to have lunch with my friend. I apologized that I couldn't have lunch with Marty's parents, but I took them to Target and promised that we'd have plenty of together time in the month they'd be in town.

That night Marty seemed off. We were in our bedroom when I finally asked him, "What's going on with you?"

"Nothing," he said.

"Okaaaaay."

"I can't believe that you would desert my parents," he said. "You are more concerned with having lunch with your friends. You don't even do the laundry on the weekend. You don't cook."

Marty launched into a list of grievances. I don't know if his parents said something about me leaving them, or if he just felt like I wasn't acting like the wife they envisioned for him. I just knew he was mad. And so was I.

"Do your parents understand that I work sometimes eighty hours a week and you work part-time so you can do your screenwriting?" I said. "Do your parents understand any of that?"

I felt so bad just putting it out there, but I wanted to get the facts straight. He left the room. I had asked him what was going on with him, and I had my answer. *Oh there's a lot going on, Chrissy,* I said to myself.

We waited to speak about it until his parents left. Meanwhile we pretended nothing was wrong. It all came out the night of a birthday party for my friend's boyfriend. He'd invited us out, and Marty alluded to not wanting to go.

"You don't have to go," I said, "but you are my husband and people are gonna ask where you are. And it will be weird if you don't come, because you've been to so many other events with these people."

"Hanging out with actors is exhausting," he said. "They're narcissistic and selfish. They make it all about themselves and they talk over each other."

I wondered if Marty was really trying to say how he felt about me. He did come to the restaurant for the birthday dinner, and we had a miserable time. I could tell he wanted to be anywhere but there, and that he felt everything I did was wrong. We barely spoke driving home. When we got home, I sat on one end of the couch. He sat on the other.

"Are you unhappy?" I asked. "Something's going on."

He didn't say a word. I was calm, but I felt this whirling inside me. This was really happening.

"Why don't you get your ring fixed so you can wear it?" I asked. "You could just get it resized."

"Ugh."

"You can take time to spend weeks going through entire record stores to find the most obscure rap album ever created by man or woman, but you can't find somebody to size your ring for you. You don't want to. Obviously, you don't want to wear it."

"No. That's not true. I'm fine."

"No, you're not," I said. "If you don't want to be with me, why don't you just tell me? I'm not an idiot. There's something wrong and you're not telling me."

"What are you talking about? Everything is about you," he said. "Chrissy, you are as narcissistic as you are selfish. From the very beginning, everything has been about you."

It felt like a slap. "From the beginning?"

"Yes."

"Well, if you've always been that unhappy," I said, "we

should probably not be together anymore. Maybe we should just separate."

"How can you be so clinical about all this?"

"You don't want to be with me. That's the bottom line. I know you don't."

"What?"

"You're being so critical and I have apparently made you miserable for like . . . years? That's not right." I reached for my support-group language. "You need to examine that and your feeling of worthiness, because it . . . it . . ." *It what, Chrissy? What?* "It takes two to tango," I finally said.

"I don't want to separate," he said.

"Will you go to counseling?" I asked.

"No, it's too American."

And there was my answer. I didn't know how to be married, apparently, and now I had to learn how to be separated. In the moment, I thought, *Oh, now I have to tell everybody that we're getting separated.* But then I realized that it didn't matter. Real failure would be staying in a relationship that made us miserable. But for Marty, he had come across the world, married this woman, and he felt like a failure. I tried to tell him that—even through all the pain—it doesn't matter what everybody else thinks. It matters how you feel in your life and in your happiness.

I wanted to at least do a better job at being an ex-wife than I did as a wife. We moved out of the apartment we were renting and into separate places. You have the TV; I'll take the couches.

And so it went.

Just after Marty and I separated, Grams got very sick. We were told she had leukemia, and that she didn't have long to live. I flew to Florida to be with her, just as my California life was dissolving.

I didn't tell her about Marty. I knew she would worry, and I wanted that time to be about her and holding her hand. I couldn't process losing her and losing Marty at the same time.

"Are you sure you're okay, honey?" she asked me.

"I'm fine," I said. "I am so fine to be sitting here with you. So fine."

That was also my answer to my family, though I told them we were separating. "We're friends," I said. That part was true. "I'm fine." That part, not so much. I didn't ask my mom for advice on how to handle the separation. I was afraid to ask what she really thought because I didn't want to hear that she had known something I didn't. I was already feeling bad enough about becoming another statistic. I just said to myself, *Figure it out, Chrissy.*

When Grams passed, I just never wanted to accept it. I think I am still in denial that she is not a phone call away. I held it together at the funeral until we sang. The song was "On Eagle's Wings," her favorite hymn, which became mine from my lonely Sundays going to church as a teen. We had to move her belongings out of her home, so my sisters and I went over to help my mom. She wanted me to have some of Grams's costume jewelry, but the thing that means the most to me is Grams's Maybelline eyeliner that I took. It's just so her and I am never giving it up.

I regret that she died before I was in a position to help her financially. I would have loved to help her buy a home, with a washer and dryer that would have made her life so much easier. She'd lived on her own or with us for the thirty years she was separated from my grandfather. There must have been so many times she felt adrift.

Now it was my turn, and I wanted to handle the divorce in the most caring, healthy way possible. Marty and I went to the notary public together for the divorce paperwork. Under fluorescent lights, we sat across from each other and signed the papers. And we both cried, sad about the end.

We are friends and text regularly. He is still writing and lives in Los Angeles. He has moved on. Recently, after we'd been divorced four and a half years, he admitted one regret.

"I'm sorry that we didn't try counseling," he said.

"Okay," I said. Me too.

He's really such a wonderful human being that people ask me, "Would you ever get back with him?" We're just not the right fit. But I love him, and I am always checking in on him.

I am still working on my goal of being a better ex-wife than I was wife. When I share my story, people sometimes wait for the "Ugh. *Him.*" It will never come. Marty is such a great guy and I am grateful that we had our time together. If you *do* hate your ex, I'd like you to consider the damage you might be doing to yourself. Look, I have heard some horror stories from my girlfriends. Things I would never tell my friends to just forgive and forget. But I think you can focus on letting go of hating someone first and then forgive the person on your own time. Because carrying hate is a heavy load, but offering forgiveness is freeing.

my new vows

When my relationship with my husband ended, I had to re-move my ego from the equation and just ask, "What was my part in that?" My ex told me I was narcissistic and selfish. That was really, *really* hard for me to process because I always thought I was the opposite. I wasn't confident enough to even think about being selfish. I had to evaluate what I was lacking and not understanding about myself, and how I could make things better in my next relationship. Therefore, I made a few vows:

1. IT'S JUST A TOWEL.

I vow to really sit with my feelings and not be impulsive in communicating them. If someone I care about leaves a wet towel on the floor of the bathroom instead of hanging it up, my first instinct is to complain about it. I need to look at why it bothers me. Is it because my mom ingrained in me that I was supposed to hang up the wet towel or I'd be in trouble? Perhaps I am projecting that on him. Or is the towel somehow representative of other things I've asked him to do that he didn't follow through on, and so this is the safe way to vent? Maybe I simply don't want to have wet towels on the floor. "Hey, it's wet," I could say calmly, without all this baggage. "Can you just hang it up?"

2. GET DOWN OFF THE CROSS.

The whole idea that you suffer for love just doesn't work. Who wants to be around that? I vow to put myself first and get down off the cross. I'm not saying you don't compromise or choose battles, but you should be willing to put yourself first so you don't burn out.

3. ASK AND RECEIVE.

I pledge to communicate my needs and my wants—and have the wisdom to know the difference (and the self-worth to ask for both). That is hard, because you might find yourself thinking, "Am I greedy? Am I unrealistic?" Yes, if you expect a diamond ring every month. Okay, that's ridiculous. But if it's a routine date night, or having a shared activity that you do for fun, let your partner know. Because if you don't tell your partner what will make you happy, you are unfairly holding that person responsible for failing to give it to you. And, when your partner gives you something, whether it's time, love, or something material, acknowledge it and tell him or her why it makes you happy.

Ask for information. You can say, "If you're feeling a certain way, I'd love to talk about it." Don't say, "I can tell you're mad at me." Because maybe it's not about you. (I know. Preposterous, right?) Let your partner decide how he or she feels, and give your partner the space to think about how to present his or her facts. Which leads to . . .

4. JUST THE FACTS.

Let's say you asked someone to take out the trash. And every day you come home to a full can. Don't say, "That makes me feel . . ." Nope, keep the feelings out of it and state the issue without any emotion. "I did the laundry the last week, and I needed help with the trash." That's the facts, honey. And way more effective than, "I do everything around here and I asked you to do one simple thing." That one always leads to a fight.

5. HE'S NOT MY BEST FRIEND, HE'S MY BOYFRIEND.

My friend Donnie and I were twin souls in a former life because we are so alike. He's the person who annoys me so much when we're together that I want to punch him in his face, but I still love him and want him around me.

I can't expect that a boyfriend is gonna act like Donnie. First, Donnie is a gentleman who prefers gentlemen. Second, as my best friend, Donnie can read my mind. With my boyfriends, I prefer to keep a little mystery.

6. REPEAT AFTER ME: "PLEASE, GOD, LET ME COME FROM A PLACE OF LOVE."

Something happens when you say those words out loud. Something shifts, and you can think about your intention in any interaction. Whenever you have an issue in a relationship, whether it be with a loved one or a family member, just check yourself and make sure you are coming from a place of love. Because you love this person, right? Your core impulse is to love, so honor that, and don't drown it out with too much talk.

This can be scary, because once you realize all anyone wants is to be loved and respected, then you realize you have to look at rivals, enemies, coworkers—anyone, really—from a place of love. Um, that's work. But it's totally worth it.

7. JUST TRY.

When I was married, I was so afraid of trying new things. I didn't even want to cook, for fear that my husband wasn't going to like what I made. If that happened, I would just fall apart, because here I was exhausted from work and I had set aside time and . . . anyway. But if I had flipped that around, and Marty cooked me dinner or planned a date for me, wouldn't that have made me happy? Whenever I think of anyone taking time to do something for me, what I cherish is not the actual thing, but the thought and intention that went into it.

This fear of trying extends to overtures of affection. I don't just mean sex; I mean looking someone in the eye and saying why you are in it to win it with that person. Why you want to share this life with the person. Our ego gets in the way and tells us that we'll look cheesy at best and at worst, the affection will not be returned. No one wants to experience the emotional version of being left hanging in a high-five. But trust me, if you put yourself out there, chances are, your feelings will be reciprocated, or at least received with kindness.

eleven

WHEN YOU'RE
SO THIRSTY YOU'RE
DEHYDRATED

Right after my divorce, it felt like every man I spoke to was interested and flirting with me. Which was ironic, because I thought that I was completely unlovable after Marty and I broke up. These guys did not treat me the way I wanted or deserved to be treated, but sometimes we want people to like us even if we don't like *them*. Whether it was my thirst or theirs, it was real.

At that time in my life, it was like I was in a romantic comedy that was way more comedy than romance. Nowadays, when my girlfriends and I start trading stories about the men we've dated, hooked up with, or dodged, I always win when it comes to the most outrageous. If I have had enough cocktails, I will even tell the toilet story. Oh dear God. Now, I'll share some of my finest dating moments with you. You've been warned.

THE SNEAKY SNEAKER SALESMAN

There was this one guy I met at a sport shop, and we flirted as he helped me try on sneakers. He was really cute, with an olive complexion and dark hair.

He took me to the register to ring me up. "If you need any more help with anything," he said, "just pop in."

"You went above and beyond," I said, thinking, *Okay. Cuuut*e.

As he went to hand me my receipt, he said, "Do you need this?"

"No, I'm good."

"Then can you write your number on it and give it to me?"

"Oh," I said. "Oh. Okay." *Play on, playah.*

He started texting me right away and was very nice, but something gave me the feeling he was in a relationship. I knew he at least had a son. Plus, that receipt move? He had that down on lock, and that takes practice. The more I got to know him, the more the red flags started popping up. Plus, he would text a lot, then stop suddenly, and then out of nowhere start again. But did I mention he was as cute as I was lonely? Yeah. There was that.

When he returned from another one of his texting sabbaticals, I'd get a message like: "Hey sexy."

"Nope," I would say, staring at the phone. "This isn't okay." Then I would text him right back. I was so, as my friends and I say, *thirsty*. For attention. Dehydrated kind of thirsty. Even as I typed out some flirty response, I would think, *Chrissy, he doesn't deserve your time. What are you doing?*

The store where he worked was near my house, so I went there multiple times to "browse," but I was browsing for him. I pictured running into him and planned exactly what I would say. "Wow, so weird! I didn't think you were gonna be here." Thank God, he never was. It was not cute. It looked like I was casing the joint on some recon mission. Hiding behind the damn soccer shin guards.

Since I never saw him, I called the store. I know! The worst! A woman answered and I asked if I could speak to him.

"He actually got transferred to the Santa Clarita store," she said flatly, like maybe she'd gotten this call a couple of times.

"Oh, thank you," I said, sounding distracted, like I was a bill collector crossing off a lead. "Have a good day!" I thought to myself, *Hmm, that's a thirty-minute drive . . .* But that was too much even for me at the time.

Honey, if you think you are humming "Desperado" now, wait for this: I did that thing you do when you act like you meant to text someone else. Wait, you haven't done that? Anyway, I texted him as if I were replying to someone asking me out:

"Yeah, I'm available on Tuesday night."

I waited a minute before typing, "So sorry, that wasn't for you."

The bait worked and we started texting again. Now I look back and I see this woman who had so much to offer somebody, and she was lurking in a sports store and doing Scooby-Doo shenanigans to get a text back. Desperation and boredom will do that to you. I finally stopped texting him back, but only once I had another guy interested. Like I said, the thirst was real.

THE ONE WHO RAN AWAY (LITERALLY)

I dated a guy for a minute who was sort of afraid for us to be seen together.

So, I'll let that sink in.

This was a few years ago, so don't judge me. By the way, he's the one that hit on *me*, I will have you know. We're in the same industry, and we were both at an event. I had just finished talking to a friend when this tall, thin guy came up to me.

"Hi," he said.

"Hi there," I said.

He told me his name. "I know who you are," I said. I'm

not ashamed to say I looked him up and down. He is sexy, a former athlete, but I didn't think he was coming on to me. It's not that I just assume no man ever wants to hit on me; it's just that I didn't think it was happening here.

"Have you eaten dinner?" he asked.

This seemed like such an odd question. Why would he care? "Uh, yeah, I ate before I came," I said.

"Oh, okay," he said, adding, after a pause as he moved closer, "Well, maybe I should take you to dinner sometime."

"Um, yeah sure, whatever," I said. That is literally what I said. Don't tell me I don't got game.

He took out his phone to take my number and I saw kids on the home screen. "Oh, you're married with kids?" I said. "How cute!"

"No, I'm divorced with kids."

That's not uncommon in LA, so that wasn't a disqualifier. Our first date was fun and he was charismatic. We had a good time, and we laughed a lot. But he seemed aggressive. I am very particular about that. I have enough aggressiveness to show interest and go in for the kiss, but don't assume I am going to kiss you back. I want you to want to kiss me, but not be angry if I don't kiss you. That's just gross.

It turned out he was, let's just say, a selfish lover. And nobody wants that. I didn't take him seriously, because I am not fantasizing about getting serious with a selfish lover, thank you very much. Still, we kept seeing each other and hooking up. We enjoyed each other's company and liked the same movies and shows, so dating him was just kind of something to do. I was on sexual autopilot.

Then one day we were on the couch at his place and out of the blue he told me, "You know, I'm not over my ex-girlfriend."

"Oh, okay," I said, totally nonplussed. Honestly, this was a no-strings thing, so I took it as him saying, "I can't eat shellfish." I simply replied, "Don't worry. It's not like I want to be in a relationship."

His head kinda cocked. "Okay," he said, but I could tell he didn't believe me.

"Okay," I said, nodding my head and seeing his one cocked head with two raised eyebrows. Boo-boo, nobody said they wanted to be in a relationship here. And, to repeat, he was also a bit of a selfish lover. I'm not sitting at home writing "Mrs. Selfish Lover" over and over in my diary.

We saw each other another couple of times for a bite, and that was fun. But then one time we stopped at the grocery store on the way to his house. As soon as we got inside, he started walking way ahead of me. When I caught up, he would move left. If I moved to the left, he'd shift right over to the right. Those athlete skills were coming in handy. It's one thing to say, "I'm just going to the chip aisle—be right back." But I knew *exactly* what he was doing.

"This mother . . ." I said under my breath. I was pissed. This guy was ashamed to be seen with me. We were driving my car—and did I mention we were driving my car because his ass didn't have one? I should have told him to Uber home from Whole Foods. And you know what I did? I parked the car at his place and sat there waiting for him to get out.

"What's wrong?" he said.

Without making eye contact, I said, "Nothing." Sure, this was no-strings, but it occurred to me I had never met a single one of his friends. He had made it clear that our hooking up wasn't something he really wanted to tell anybody about. I had been fine with that at the time, but it suddenly seemed kind of twisted. Like he was ashamed to be seen with me. Fuck. That. I wanted to bolt and he could tell. I deserved better than a man who was ashamed of me.

"No really," he pressed, "what's wrong?"

"I just think it's kinda shitty how you treated me in the grocery store."

"I don't know what you're talking about," he said in that exasperated lying voice men use when they know exactly what you're talking about.

"Okay, I think I'm just gonna, um, go home."

He called me a couple of times after that night and I ignored him. Finally, I relented. His opening line was, "I don't want you to feel I was doing anything intentionally."

Ummm, okay.

"But you were. You were embarrassed to be seen with

me. Even if you were subconsciously embarrassed, it was apparent."

He apologized and I admit, all was forgiven. I hung in. You know, what you do when you're bored or making shitty decisions. Over the next five months, we went out every now and then. Casual dating was a new experience for me, so I wasn't sure if this was dating or hooking up. He would always pay. He even ordered for me, and not in a creepy way where it was like women should be seen and not heard. I thought it was a date. Looked like a date. Felt like a date. This just in: it wasn't a date. Does anyone know what a date looks like? 'Cause if you do, could you let me know?

Then a few months later I met someone else, someone who I was more invested in getting to know better. So, I called our elusive shopper one last time.

"Listen, I met this guy and I am interested in him," I told him. "I am just letting you know that I don't really want to do this anymore."

"Wait, what?"

I tried saying it slower. "I don't want to just hook up anymore. I am interested in this guy emotionally, not just physically."

There was a long pause. I even checked my phone to see if the call dropped.

"But like," he said, "I really like you."

"Unh-huh," I said, supercasual. "Okay."

"But *you*," he said. "As a human being. Like, I *love* you."

"Oh? Yeah, okay."

Five months prior it had been "I don't want to be in a relationship" and keep-away in the damn grocery store. Then it's "But, I love you"!

Maybe it was just about his ego being bruised. People want to play with their toys. And I was taking his toy away. Isn't it funny how when a toy gets taken away, it's the only one we want to play with? We always want what we can't have.

Here's the thing: two people can have an intimate relationship and be friends. It can be casual and fun and noncommittal, as long as both people are good with that. In that scenario, I never thought *he'd* be the one catching feelings. Because he had set the ground rules. I was just playing with the rules I was given. When you set your own rules, you can say, "No, I am not going to allow people to treat me this way." The whole point of that relationship was for me to communicate my boundaries—even just with myself—and say what works for me and what doesn't.

THE MILE-HIGH SOLDIER

I was sitting in the window seat on an airplane when I met him. Back then I was a little self-conscious about my size in those coach seats. As a big girl, you are often made to feel like you are taking up too much space, and airplanes aren't fun for anyone.

"Oh my God, am I squishing you?" I asked the man next to me in the two-seater.

"No." He paused. "And it's okay if you touch me."

And we're off. This guy was very flirty right out of the gate. We were on a five-and-a-half-hour flight from Orlando to Los Angeles, so he had time to workshop all his pickup lines on me. He said he was going to boot camp and then heading off to Iraq. My sister Monica and I had just gotten tattoos, with mine being a little anchor on the inside of my wrist. Soldier Boy kept using it as an excuse to touch my arm. Making that bod contact. He was a sturdy boy, about twenty-four. Okay, maybe twenty-three. His cropped hair had grown out a bit, and there was something very mature and sexually confident about him. He raised his pant leg to show me his tattoo of an eagle.

"You can touch it," he said. I laughed, and he said, "I'm going to be really lonely for a really long time." He mentioned this more than once, and about an hour into our conversation, he did this little thing with his eyes, drawing my attention to the airplane bathroom.

I was honestly baffled. Well, atten*tion*! I thought he was joking. But he was so convincing in his confidence that I seriously thought, *I should do it for my country, right?* I come from a military family. I know what sacrifices must be made, and here was this poor kid leaving his entire family and everything that he has ever known and he couldn't be more than, what, twenty-two?

Then I thought about how I can barely fit in that bath-room. And I realized that it was ridonculous that I was even having this conversation with myself. I couldn't do that with this twenty-two-year-old I had just met. This *maybe* twenty-one-year-old soldier boy . . . Okay, I am not sure he was old enough to drink. Vote, yes. Drink, no.

When we landed, it was as if the spell was broken, at least for me. But our soldier fought on. He told me where the gate for his connection was, like he was inviting me to his hotel room. "Come on by Terminal 6 . . ." Where did this guy think we were going to affirm our love for this country?

"Listen," I said. "I want you to know I appreciate your service and I will be thinking of you."

I could tell that's when he realized I wasn't going to go above and beyond to show my support for the troops. "It was really nice meeting you," I said.

"You too," he said. He cocked his head one more time with those puppy-dog eyes, and I attempted to hide my blush. He *almost* got me.

"I'll be thinking of you," I said.

"I'll be thinking of *you*."

I have thought of that man-boy often and prayed for his safety. To all the men and women in the service, I love you. Just buy a girl dinner first, 'kay?

READY, SET . . . PSYCH!

I matched with a former-athlete reality star on the Bumble app. That's where the girls like the picture first, so they have a say in who they talk to. It was fun because it's like you're shopping, you know, for men.

He seems interesting, I thought, meaning, "hot and rich." He was a football player and I knew exactly who he was. But then when we started talking, I realized he couldn't string a sentence together. Maybe he had so many DMs open he couldn't keep us all straight.

And scene. But I thought, okay, your girl's moving up! Heeey! But then I thought, maybe not so much.

BATHROOM BLOW-UP

We met, sort of, in a grocery store at one in the morning. I was in Gainesville again, and what else do you do when you are still on California time and nothing else is open? I was on a health kick, so I was there buying vegetables and feeling all good about myself. I was also in a space of "I am not interested in men. I don't want attention. I don't care." And of course, you know what happens when you make that decision. The men, they just come out of the woodwork. It is so bizarre. I swear they can smell it on us.

While I was in the produce department I noticed this

cute young guy, who was carrying around a bag of Oreos but seemed intent on looking at the vegetables next to where I was. As I walked through the store, I noticed he happened to be looking at things in the same aisles as me, but I didn't think much of it. Then when I went to pay, he was right behind me. Still, we didn't talk to each other.

I got in my car, and I saw him exit the store and scan the parking lot. I thought he was looking for where he'd parked, but then he kicked off on a skateboard toward my car.

Oh. Okay. Grown man on a skateboard. That's so edgy and cute.

As I pulled out of the parking lot and made a left, Mr. Skateboarder was right next to me, loudly saying, "Excuse me."

My first thought was, *Oh God, did I almost hit him?* I was stopped in the middle of the road.

I blurted out, "I'm so sorry, I didn'—"

He stood there, skateboard in one hand, Oreos in the other. "I saw you in the store—"

We spoke over each other, once, then again. Finally, he blurted out, "I just think you're really beautiful."

"Oh," I said, surprised. "Thanks." We were then caught in this long, awkward moment, which I chose to make more awkward.

"You know, I don't live here," I said. "I live in Los Angeles."

"Cool, I used to live in LA," he said. "I was sponsored." He kicked up his board and added, "I was a professional skateboarder."

"Hence the skateboard."

"Yes," he said. "Hence the skateboard."

I had nothing else to do while I was in Gainesville. "Oh, so are you gonna call me?" I asked.

"I would love your number," he said.

He called, and a couple of nights later we went out for pizza and played pool at a dive bar. Yes, my first college experience! Finally! We fed each other pizza at the bar, and I tried to be as sexual as possible. I was really trying to turn him on.

Now, I'm going to ask you to go on the rest of this date with me. It isn't pretty. But, I promise you'll laugh or cringe. Deal?

So. Mr. Skateboard bought me a beer and I thought about how my stomach can get a little, uh, active when I mix pizza and beer. I don't drink beer and I am delusional about not being lactose intolerant, but hey, when in college . . .

He lived close to the bar and as grown adults do, we walked over to his place, which was tiny but cute. We kissed on the couch, which led to his bed, which led to him falling asleep. Wait, I thought I was in college. Why is he going to bed so early? Kids these days.

I decided it was time to go. Because guess what? I had the worst stomachache. The problem was that he had a door that only locked from the outside. I couldn't just walk out and leave the door unlocked, could I? But I also didn't want to wake him.

And then, that beer and pizza started talking back to me and I needed to use a bathroom immediately. STAT. "Oh my god oh my god oh my god," I whispered as I tried to extricate myself from under his arm. *This is going to be really bad. This is going to be really bad.*

Are you a classy broad or a gentle man? If so, you might want to skip to the next chapter. 'Cause I'll just be here pooping my brains out. I understand.

Still here? Everybody poops, right?

So get this: his bathroom was right next to the bed. Oh no! *Oh no!* I got out from under his arm and I ran in, barely making it in time. I was quietly blowing up his bathroom—and everyone knows you can't quietly blow up nothin'. And then I realized there was no toilet paper.

As I was trying and failing to be the silent nonstinky pooper, flushing as I went to minimize the damage, my eyes were darting about the room. There was no air freshener. Okay. Worse, he didn't even have hand soap. "What the hell?" I said.

Luckily, he had a box of Kleenex I could use—

"Chrissy?"

He was calling my name. This man who set me up with pizza and beer and no toilet paper or soap was calling my name.

"Hi!" I yelled. "Just a minute." *Missy, why didn't you keep driving? You should have said nothing to this man. Why wasn't the skateboard a deal breaker?* I cursed myself for being so friendly. And for my love of pizza.

When there seemed to be enough of a break in the action for me to get up, I decided that I would use some of his shampoo to wash my hands. Desperate times, honey, desperate times. I put some shampoo in the toilet to mask the smell and hide the poop streaks. Now that we are real friends, I can tell you streaks are never in! Not in your hair, not in the toilet.

And, when I went in for the final flush, I got nothing. The damn thing was going to overflow.

"Don't do this to me," I begged.

"Chrissy, are you okay?"

"By all that is holy," I whispered, desperately grabbing his plunger. "Flush, please, flush."

Finally, it did. I needed to use the shampoo to wash my hands a second time and opened the door. And it was clear . . . that Skateboarder. Had. Heard. Everything.

"I'm gonna go," I said.

I had already gone. But we both knew it.

"Okay," he said, looking absolutely *bewildered*.

Once I made it to the car, I just burst out laughing. Whether from relief or disbelief, I honestly laughed all the way home.

Thank you for hanging in. I know that was a bit over

the top. It was crazy embarrassing. But I have a friend who literally sends her husband out to the store when she has to poop. That's not healthy. I have vowed to never be that woman.

I wouldn't advise you to blow up the toilet on the first date. But if you do, and you're still together, that person is a keeper. Don't we all want someone who accepts all we have to offer?

don't call him back

"If you could go back in time, what advice would you give yourself in your twenties?"

I was onstage at CurvyCon, a plus-size fashion conference held during New York Fashion Week. I am sure people expected me to make some deep philosophical statement, but the answer, to me, was so simple.

"Don't call him back," I said immediately. *"Don't call him back!* He does not deserve you. You're smarter and prettier and like . . . what?"

The audience went crazy laughing, because we've all been there, right? Okay, I won't make assumptions about you, but I know that in my life there have been times when I was so desperate for validation that I thought I could only find it in a man. I was always looking for it outside of myself, but having beauty and confidence is an inside job. Still, that outside affirmation is just too hard to resist sometimes—and it can make you settle for less because you want attention, no matter what that entails.

Dating is so confusing. But especially in Los Angeles. There's a consensus here that people are always working an agenda. And also, it's the land of the Pretty, which doesn't make it easier. Remember how back in the day, when a woman didn't want to go out with a man or wanted to play hard-to-get, she would say, "Oh, I have to wash my hair." It's such a boss thing to say. "Not only am I not interested . . . but you aren't even worthy of a good excuse." I miss those old-school traditions. Back then you waited for a man to call you; you didn't call him. Or text him, which is more the norm now. Technology has made people socially inept and eliminated the need to get to know someone. It used to be that if you met somebody at a bar or a meetup group and you were attracted to the person and vibing, you'd say, "Let's trade phone numbers." You'd go out on a date and it would be going great, but then you'd find out he has a cat. You might say to yourself, "Ugh, I don't really love that, but he's great, so . . . okay."

But online you see that someone's profile says, "Love cats," and *swipe*. There's such an influx of men and women at our fingertips that no one has to get to know you. You can be minimized down to your pet preference.

"Look at his shoes."

Swipe.

"Why is his hair like that?"

Swipe.

"He cropped someone out. Who was that?"

Swipe.

People are scrolled through like cattle. And what is the incentive for someone to treat you right when the person can swipe left at any second?

So now, I have a new system I keep reminding myself of by sharing it with my friends. It's based on the acronym HALT, used in self-care in cases of depression. "Girlfriend, before you text him, ask yourself: Are you hungry? Are you angry? Are you lonely? Are you tired?! HALT! HALT! HALT! Don't text him if the answer is yes to any of those questions!" Because I know well from my own dating experience that I need to ask myself if I genuinely like this person or if I am trying to fill a void because I am frustrated in my life about something, or simply lonely.

It does not help me that I tend to attract men who are needy. I'm not necessarily out to fix them; at least I don't put out that vibe. I thought it was bad luck, but then I heard Oprah define the Law of Attraction on her show: "Like attracts like."

Hold on, I thought. *What does that say about me? If the energy that I am putting out is what I am attracting, then am I needy?* I don't want to be needy. I don't want to be a mess. I don't want to use somebody. Because the men I had been with in my life—they had all possessed some degree of these traits. All those relationships, I was accumulating research. *Wait, this is weird. What do you mean this has happened ten times? And the common denominator was what? Me?*

Obviously, that didn't make me feel good. But I share these stories because maybe somebody can relate to them, and I don't want them to happen again. It's hard to change relationship habits. You can't move a rooted tree overnight. You have to dig deep, and it's still something that I work on. Because you constantly make compromises in relationships. And not just in romantic relationships—any kind of relationship.

Now I want to be with people who want to better themselves, because I want to be my best self. When you develop true confidence and self-esteem, you don't just settle for someone who is willing to take you out, or sleep with you. Because you should decide who to spend your time with based on what you get from that person, and how the person fits into the life you want for yourself. Because time is something you can't get back once you lose it. You spend that with someone who doesn't deserve that gift you are giving him, and you will never be able to get that back.

I believe it's okay to step back and look at your relationships from a selfish perspective. We are conditioned, especially women, to invest time and care into others first. What are you getting in return? People are always showing you who they are and what they think of you. Pay attention to how someone treats you, and if you feel undervalued, then tell him, "Boy, 'bye."

When you haven't had a lot of experience dating, you learn things slower and later in life. I know I did. I look at my girlfriends who don't have to want for a date any night of the week, and I see how they've honed their standards. They can suss out a loser in the first ten minutes of a date. If you feel as if you have your pick, when you have confidence and know you are desirable, you don't settle. But if you don't have much opportunity, or you haven't so far, it is harder to make those calls. That said, I sometimes think the universe helps you dodge bullets. If you're not currently dating, there's a reason why, and it's probably for your own good.

When you are discovering who you are at a core level, you are dodging all the bullets anyway. If I can leave you with one thing, it's that you don't need to call him back or pick up your phone. Because you don't need a man.

twelve

FALLING FORWARD

I was a talent agent for nine years, and for an embarrassing amount of that time, I was just going through the motions. My commute was two hours each way, so I lived either at my desk or in a car. All I thought about was my clients' needs. January would slip into summer, and then it would be another December of eating holiday Sprinkles cupcakes gifted by actors. Year after year would go by without me pursuing my acting or singing career in any way. Deep down I still wanted to entertain, to relate, to love through art. It was something I had to do, a desire placed upon my heart. I just didn't know how.

I believe firmly that you're never given a vision without a provision. You have a destiny, and you are also given the tools to get there. I had this ability to share, but I was keeping it to myself. I distinctly remember stopping at a light one day and having a conversation with myself. I didn't want to be an agent anymore. It wasn't fulfilling me. I was grateful to help people on their journey, but I was getting more and more depressed watching people start their dream lives with such excitement. I didn't resent them, really, but my work no longer fulfilled me.

"But you're good at it," I said out loud, as the light turned green.

That was usually enough to stop me, but then I thought, *Well, of course I'm successful as an agent. That's all I do!*

I decided I needed to see a life coach. The thing about getting a life coach is they're great to have, but when you really need one you can't afford one. So, I saved up for one session.

When the time came, I got right to it, about wanting to be a singer or actress but feeling stuck in my role as an agent. Even if I did quit being an agent, I wasn't getting auditions and I couldn't imagine money being even tighter than it already was with my little paycheck.

"What are you doing to stay ready for when an opportunity comes?" the coach asked.

I had no answer. I was at work all day. I was part of the industry, but I wasn't doing anything to work on my craft.

"Chrissy, if you're not willing to invest in yourself— whether it's acting classes or exercise or eating right—invest in yourself and your brand and your person and your acting, how do you expect anyone else to do that? Why would a network invest in you if you're not willing to?"

He was right. Life coaches are life coaches for a reason, I guess. But it was more than that. I wasn't even cultivating who I was as a person then. I wasn't doing anything to stay ready for an acting or singing opportunity or even a chance to grow as a person.

I was at my desk as usual, and there was this brief lull when the phones weren't ringing and I had returned all my calls for the day. In that quiet, I took the time to think. I decided that I had to at least try to be ready. I had gotten into the habit of staying at the office ridiculously late. I needed to stop that. So, I found a weeknight acting class. It wouldn't be the end of the world if I left work at 7 p.m. for an 8 p.m. class. The office wouldn't fall apart and it wasn't going to impact my work. I was worth that small investment.

I also found voice lessons I could take on weekends at Dot Todman's studio in Culver City. Dot is a vocal empowerment coach, and a sort of therapist. From the very first class with her, I realized I was afraid of my own voice. I spoke all the time about wanting to be a singer, but when it came to showcasing my voice, my ego and fear of being vulnerable got in the way. I learned that good singing was not just about the voice, the instrument, but also your mind, your soul, and your body. Dot said that if your mind is not in a good place, you're not ready to sing, and the way you sing is the way you see the world. Meanwhile, I had become afraid of my own shadow.

To help me rediscover my voice, Dot had me do homework, such as singing to myself naked in the mirror. "You have to just be comfortable with being yourself," she told me. I had to attain comfort before I could get to learning about voice and technique.

Letting go of the need for perfection, in singing and in life, allowed me freedom to improve. When I sang for people, I learned, I was doing so to have a good time and share with others, not to be perfect. In those weekend courses, at the karaoke nights with the class and the showcases we put on, I gradually grew more confident.

As I was taking the acting class and Dot's vocal lessons, I grew happier. Living stressed out and unfulfilled had closed me off to the next chapter. I wasn't excited at work, or in my dating life; I'd settled with the now. But, when I took steps toward something new, I felt stronger and connected within myself. I just naturally had a lot more to give to other people and I didn't expect anyone else to make me happy. Because *I* was making me happy.

More importantly, I was sending out a signal of intention. I am a firm believer that what you do and what you spend your time doing is a message to the universe. And the universe doesn't know good or bad; it just knows what you are focusing on.

It's interesting how you just make a tiny—or big—shift,

and the universe conspires with you. Not long after I started this new investment plan, I got what I was certain would be my big break, a recurring role on *American Horror Story: Freak Show.*

We'll get to that later, but first I want to talk about you. At the beginning of this book, I asked you to think about what request you want to put out to the universe. Now I want to ask what message you want to send to the universe.

Let's do this. Visualize a perfect day of doing what you love. Seriously, wake up in the bed you dream of, at whatever time you want. What are the sheets like? Who's there? It's okay if it's just you, so feel free to dream. Now get up to start the day. Think about what your perfect day of meaningful work entails. For me, that is full of connecting to people using art. For my older sister Monica, I know that connection comes from nurturing people, most likely through her amazing baking skills. That is personal, and only you can know what your meaningful work will be.

Now, what do you have to do to get ready for that perfect day? Not how you'll get there, but what you will need to be able to do that work to the best of your ability. Nothing happened for me until I invested in my craft. So, ask yourself what you need to invest in. If the main obstacle is money, and believe me, I get that, look to see if there are ways for you to get around, under, or over it. "I can't afford school" is not the same as "I applied for a scholarship."

Just like "I wish I could own a bakery" is not the same

as "I checked with the bakery I love and they need early morning help. I can see what it's like to work in a bakery this way." Or how "I really want to be an actor" is not the same as "I went to an acting class and I met someone I can partner with in self-producing material on my phone."

So, you set the intention, but you have to do the work to be ready. Don't let people talk you out of your success, because many people are conditioned to have lowered expectations about what life can offer. If you're from a town where everyone is a bricklayer or a miner and you want to make music, it sounds ridiculous to them. They can't think in bigger and broader strokes.

And don't let your fear of success stop you, either. I keep a Marianne Williamson quote in my heart. C'mon, quote! "Our deepest fear is not that we are inadequate. Our deepest fear is that we are powerful beyond measure." That always got me. We are not taught that we are limitless and fantastic just the way we are. We are told, "You're not enough," and "You're too much of this."

Being who you are is enough. You don't have to become a success, because you already are one. Let go of your fear and dare to be your greatest, truest self. Because the world needs you.

thirteen

THE NOT-SO-BIG EASY

I was sitting at my desk, reviewing a contract for a client, when I saw a text pop up from a friend who was an agent I used to work with. Here's the text chain:

> **Girl, there is a role for you!**

> **!!!**

> **But I think for the first time in your life, you're gonna feel like you're not big enough for something.**

> **What is it?!**

> **Send it over!**

She emailed me the "sides," which is the term used for a small portion of a script used in the audition.

Ping!

I read the bold print in the subject line and my heart flipped—and then sank.

I called her right away.

"*American Horror Story*? I'm not gonna get that. Please."

"Chrissy, there is something about it. I think you will get it."

"Hey, if you can get me an audition I will go, of course. But I mean, are you kidding? Ryan Murphy?"

As I read the sides, I wondered why they sounded so familiar. Then I realized they were Sarah Paulson's lines from *Coven*, the previous season of *AHS*. The show was so careful about what they leak out into the world, especially about a new season, that actors don't get the real sides for the character ahead of an audition. All I knew was that I'd be playing a big girl from an affluent home, a Park Avenue princess from the Upper East Side of Manhattan. And she really enjoyed eating. She liked being a big girl, but never felt she fit in with her rich, thin family.

I got it, except for the rich part.

I wanted this role bad, so I got to work. First of all, I had to land the audition. I knew my friend thought I would be right for the role and I trusted her, so I gave that up to the universe because it was out of my hands.

Then, I had to plan my look for the audition (because

I knew I was going to get the chance). The story was set in the 1950s, so I thought about a dress I had in my closet, a halter neck with a cute little tie and a sweater to go with it. The character was affluent, so I was sure she had nice clothes and I had to make sure I looked put together.

The day of the audition, I did my hair in a little '50s flip and I think I even wore a headband. I went to the audition on my lunch break, and when I walked in I saw that every girl in the waiting room was wearing contemporary street clothes. And of course, I saw the one actress who is sort of my arch-nemesis. For real, she couldn't be lovelier, but she books a lot of the jobs that I don't get. I see her at every audition. Every single one. This is how our conversations always go.

"Hi."

"Hi."

Annnd that's about it.

Seriously, she's great and she deserves all her success. But I really, really wanted this job, y'all.

Looking around the room, I felt like I stood out because of my outfit, but I decided that was a good thing. I am not saying I am better than these great actors, but for me personally, I needed to do everything to prove I was right for the role.

I knew that they wanted to cast the biggest woman that they could find. So, I wasn't shocked that when the casting director's first question when I walked in was, "How much do you weigh?"

"Well, what do you want?" I said. "Do you want the truth?"

"I want you to give me the biggest number possible," he said.

I fudged the number up fifty, sixty, maybe even one hundred pounds. They didn't know anyone at that number personally, I told myself, so they couldn't tell if I was adding a few. Besides, this was a Ryan Murphy show. He could literally make TV magic. I had to do what I had to do.

I did the reading and there was a pause. "Okay, do you want to do that again?" the casting director said.

"Okay." And then of course my head started going crazy because I was second-guessing my character choice, and at the same time I wondered if the casting director had seen something he liked that he wanted more of. So I did it again.

"Great," he said. "You know, what about trying it another way?" He gave me a note about the delivery.

Take three, but obviously there was something about me that he liked or he wouldn't waste his time. I knew enough about auditioning to know that.

"Great, thank you."

I went to leave and when I was nearly out the door of the waiting room, I heard him behind me. "Hey, can you come back and do it again?"

Okay. My heart was beating faster.

"We just want you to try it this way," he said. I thought maybe he was giving me multiple chances because he thought, "It's in there somewhere, I just haven't seen it yet." And this fourth time might have been my last chance. They taped it, and I knew Ryan Murphy would see this.

I went straight back to work, because the audition had taken up my whole lunch break. I had to shift gears right into agent speed.

That night, I had my best friend, Donnie, over. Donnie and I came to California together from Florida, and we even used to have the same manager.

"Chrissy, this will change your life," he told me. "This will absolutely change your life."

"Don't say that until I book it," I said.

"You're gonna book it."

"Staahp, Donnie!"

A couple of days passed, and my agent called me. "They said they really like you for a role," he said.

"What does that mean?" I asked.

"Well, they're not going to do callbacks," he said. "Ryan's going to choose from tape."

Ughh. Here's the thing: So much of being an actress and being an agent is how you sell yourself in the room. I know I am good in the room. I have had clients who are better on tape, because they are not themselves in the audition room. And, who can blame them? There is nothing organic about auditioning. You are literally pretending an office is a hospital room, or acting as if you are speaking to Jessica Lange's character when Jessica Lange is nowhere to be seen but there's a twenty-seven-year-old guy sitting across from you instead. Come on.

The next day I wasn't feeling well, so I worked from home. Donnie came over to check on me, and while he was there I got another call from my agent.

"Chrissy, stand by because we are going to find out what's going on with *Horror Story*," he said.

"I thought you had news!" I said. "Y'all, don't play with my emotions today."

"So if they want to book you, we just want to make sure you are available to do a prosthetics fitting—"

"YES, YES!" I yelled. "You know that I am! I don't care if I'm sick or not. I will go anywhere I need to be."

I went back to trying to work from home, which was difficult because I was obviously distracted. Donnie and I just kept looking at my phone. And then it rang again.

"Chrissy, it's yours," my agent said.

Donnie and I, as sick as I was, went running around the house like crazy, jumping up and down. My agent heard all the screaming, and when we broke to breathe, he told me, "Okay, now you have to go get fitted for the fat suit."

Oh, how I laughed! I mean, the irony of it all. I needed a fat suit.

Off I went right to AFX Studio, a very cool prosthetic house that everyone in Hollywood uses. It's run by Dave Anderson and his wife, Heather Langenkamp Anderson— oh, yes, that's right! Nancy from the *Nightmare on Elm Street* series! They are the nicest couple and put me right at ease. Their workshop is like a horror fantasy come to life, with prototypes of monsters and ghouls above you on a top-tier shelf surrounding the whole place.

They told me I could wear a tank top and pants I didn't mind getting ruined, and for the next two hours they wrapped me in wet strips of plaster of Paris to make a body cast. The strips were warmed in hot water, and around my stomach it was fine, but as they put it on my chest it became so stifling and heavy.

"Um, what if I can't get out of this," I half-joked. "Who here is gonna help me?"

The heavier it got, the more I couldn't move. But they needed it to be accurate. Ryan wanted me to look about four hundred pounds heavier, so they needed an exact replica of me: my legs, my stomach, my back—all of me, so they could magnify each part in a way that looked true to life.

Finally, it was time to saw me out of it. They used a small saw and you'd think I would have been scared, but I was just happy to be free. They sliced it down either side of me, pulling it apart as I took deep breaths.

Then they created the suit, stuffing it with couch material. I pulled on legs with suspenders, and the top part was like a vest. The first time I put it on, I was like *Whoa*. I couldn't see my feet and I couldn't walk without waddling. It was trippy, because I know how easy it is to gain weight. This could happen.

And so, Ima Wiggles was born. That is the name Jessica Lange's character, Elsa Mars, gives the character when she recruits her from the weight-loss sanitarium Ima's been exiled to by her parents. Elsa celebrates her size, wanting Ima to join her carnival freak show. Elsa needed to keep recruiting new acts to keep filling seats. The amazing part of the role for me is that Ima didn't *want* to change or lose weight. She loved herself for who she was. She was happy. The dichotomy between her and the other freaks in the show is that she has always felt separate and less worthy. People have tried to make her feel that way, and she was like, "Whatever. I am who I am." I loved that about her.

When I was cast, I basically resigned for the leave of absence. I had to call all my clients to tell them I would be away filming for three months, and arranged for them to be covered by a colleague. The show was filming in New Orleans, and the idea of living there for free all that time seemed pretty magical. Even better was being in the amazing creative bubble that is the Ryan Murphy camp, as I soon learned. I got a master class in acting. There I was with greats like Jessica Lange, Kathy Bates, Angela Bassett, and Michael Chiklis, Evan Peters and Emma Roberts, and, oh, the lovely and amazing Sarah Paulson. Oh my God. Everyone was top-notch, from the directors to the costume designers, and both hair and makeup departments. These are absolute professionals who are revered and rewarded for their work.

And me.

Honestly, it was nerve-racking to be so much more in-experienced than these actors. I am here to tell you that if I hadn't already been working through surrendering my ego over the previous two years, I would not have made it through production. I would have quit, and written the story for myself that I was not good enough and probably given up acting all together. My own fear that I didn't deserve this would have crushed me. When you're given something good, you sometimes wait for the other shoe to drop.

I joined the show at the eighth episode mark, so not only had a lot of these people already worked together on the series, they had also been filming this season for a while. I was the new girl in school once again. My first day, I had to film a scene sitting across from Jessica Lange. You know, acting legend Jessica Lange.

Right before we started, I had to break it down to myself like this: *Okay, Chrissy. You're a woman, she's a woman. She wears pants, you wear pants. Sometimes. You both go to the bathroom. You're both human beings. Yes, you respect her and she's fantastic, but Chrissy, you gotta keep it together and do your work.*

There we were, sitting across from each other, and there is always downtime when you're shooting. The crew needs to set up different shots, move the lights, create different cov-erage. And as people were whirling around us, I remember thinking, *Do I look at her? Do I make eye contact with her?*

She is a veteran, so I decided I was going to let her sort of dictate what happened.

When we finally made eye contact, she sort of smiled at me, but not really. I wondered whether that was a character choice as the owner of the freak show. Because if you watched the show, you know how hardened her character Elsa was by life. She didn't want to get close to anybody. But it did kind of hurt my heart. Throughout the season, I was like, "Oh damn, maybe she doesn't like me." And it took me a while to realize that not everybody is going to like me— but if I am a good person and I treat people well and love myself, that's all I can do. It was hard, because who doesn't want Jessica Lange to like them? Who doesn't want *anyone* to like them?

My experience on *AHS* made me wonder if I was cut out for show business. I had to do the work of believing that I was enough and deserving of the role, and showing up for myself. Nothing was personal. Some actors wear headphones, and if they don't say hi to you in the morning it could just be that they are running lines. It's not personal.

I was by myself in New Orleans, in a hotel room, thinking, *Maybe this is not for me.* And I ate about it. Because that was another mind-fuck: I could take off the suit and feel smaller than the suit. And if I did gain weight, nobody could tell. After filming, I would always take the streetcar down to the Fresh Market and buy this chocolate-chip cookie dough without eggs in it, so you could eat it raw.

I ate so many pretzels—these little doughy baby pretzels, hard crunchy pretzels, pretzel sticks with ranch dip. And some fruit here and there. For balance.

The showrunners kept the scripts so top-secret that we never knew what was going to happen next. The production drafts were bloodred instead of the usual blue. You can't Xerox red paper—it was for security, but what a coincidence. I loved all those details. They were all new to me and so exciting.

One day, the next episode arrived and I skimmed through to make sure Ima lived to see another day. Holy shit, there it was: IMA WIGGLES SINGS HOLE'S "DOLL PARTS."

"Wait a minute," I said aloud. I dropped the script and fell in slow motion. I thought it was so brilliant, because Ima Wiggles is supposed to look like a doll. They wanted Ima to duet with Kathy Bates's character, and I learned the guitar parts for filming. I recorded the song with Kathy, who could not have been sweeter. She played Ethel Darling the Bearded Lady, and had to do such a thick Baltimore accent for her scenes that she just never stopped using it, no matter where she went. When the song was mixed, the producers emailed us both the playback and it was rad. Then we shot it, and it was amazing.

The bad news came as I was sitting alone at this faux Cheesecake Factory in New Orleans, debating whether to get the cheesecake. They were going in a different direction with the episode and needed to cut the duet.

"Got it," I said, not getting it at all but not wanting to show how disappointed I was.

As soon as I hung up, I ordered the cheesecake and called my mom.

"Mom, I can't," I said. "I don't know what to do. My heart's broken."

"I'm sorry, I'm so sorry," she said. "I know how much this meant to you."

"Yeah."

I wanted to tell her how lonely I was, but I didn't want her to worry. I wanted her to be happy for me. I was living my dream, right? Getting this job made it seem real for my mother. To be on five episodes of one of the biggest shows out there gave me validity. Maybe I did know what I was doing.

The next day, Kathy walked over to me on set. "I can't believe they took the song out," she said. "I wept. I wept when I heard that."

"Me too," I said. She understood my sadness, and was willing to be vulnerable and share that with me. What a gift she gave me!

Evan Peters was also willing to share that vulnerability with me. I walked away from one scene saying, "Ugh, that is not how I wanted it to go," heaving a sigh.

"I feel that way every day," he told me.

"Really?" I said.

"Every day," he said.

I had built up everyone around me in my head because I didn't feel like we were equals. I didn't feel worthy. But these actors were good because they were willing to work their butts off and still feel that they had to prove themselves. Someone as wonderful as Evan questioned himself, and we all do because we're human. That moment on *AHS* was pivotal for me as a human being, not just as an actress.

I later met Sylvester Stallone when he guest-starred on *This Is Us*, and he told me his secret to success in the business.

"It's all about resilience," he said. "Your thick skin. You standing in line long enough." I knew exactly what he meant. There are a lot of people who are super talented in show business, but they let other people get the better of them. I still second-guess myself, thinking I need to be like another actor. But I stop and remind myself that I am at my best when I stay authentic to who I am.

What's crazy is that when I continue to do that—show up for myself, and stay authentic—it not only helps to reassure me that I *am* good enough, but it also, I hope, inspires others to be themselves and know that they are enough just as they are.

And I have to tell you I was right not to take Julia's process personally. After *This Is Us* took off, we were both at a *Hollywood Reporter* roundtable for dramatic actresses. I was so nervous to see her again, and she could not have been kinder. I had come into the place where she worked, a new face who would be gone in a blink. Now there she was, grabbing my hand, and giving it a squeeze in a loving way. We were off duty, she was not leading a show, and she was not shooting a scene.

Oh, here comes the lesson, I thought. Back on that set, it had nothing to do with *me* at all.

I TEXTED SARAH PAULSON AFTER SHE WON HER EMMY IN 2016. SHE had been nominated for the *Hotel* season on *American Horror Story*, and won for her work as Marcia Clark on *The People v. O.J. Simpson*. She is the best—so talented but so dang funny at the same time. On the season I was on, *Freak Show*, Sarah played Bette and Dot Tattler, who were conjoined twins. She'd say to me, "Chrissy, if you are gonna be in a scene, make sure you are far away, because if you're close to me you're gonna be here allllll day." Anyone in her frame would have to do their scene twice, since she was playing twins. Each of her scenes would average twelve to fifteen hours, while the rest of us averaged only five. She was so committed to getting her role right that she would record the dialogue and wear an earpiece so that as she played Bette, she could hear Dot reacting, and vice versa. She was playing opposite herself! I am convinced Sarah can do anything.

I told her that her award was so well deserved, and she wrote me back, something to the effect of "I'm going to sit in this space of just gratitude." I was really struck by that. There aren't many times where you actually sit in that good space of being excited about where you've come from and what you've accomplished. Because in Hollywood, in any career really, and in life, it's always the next thing, and the next thing. Instead, recognize the hard work you have done, and give yourself a pat on the back for a minute. Then move on.

When I finished *American Horror Story* I felt had completed acting grad school, with all the crazy long hours to get the one perfect shot. I thought my role as Ima was going to set the stage for my new career. I was ready. I had been putting deposits in my confidence bank with my singing and acting lessons, and now this. Now I had shown up for myself when things were difficult, and it only affirmed that I was on the right path.

hurt people hurt people

Look, not everyone is gonna like us.

I know! Crazy, right? Because we're so great and awesome and funny and . . . well, sometimes none of those things matter: people have been hurt and they think they will feel better if they hurt you.

I once had a job where I worked in a group setting with some amazing people. And one of those people went out of her way to make sure that everyone knew—including me—that they were not so amazing. Don't try to figure out the identity of this person because it doesn't matter. We all have that person in our life at one point or another. You and I know it wasn't anyone in the *This Is Us* cast because as far as I am concerned, they are all gold-dipped specimens of God's grace.

Let's call this person something imaginative like X

(though the unevolved part of me would prefer the B-word). She and I travel in very different vehicles, body and mind. I would bet that she has probably been thin her whole life. She is also funny and smart and beautiful, and for whatever reason life has taught her to sharpen each one of those gifts into a weapon.

So, while we worked together, this b . . . I mean, X, made small, cutting comments whenever she was forced to be in my vicinity. She sighed, she huffed, and she turned her very essence into one giant figurative eye roll. If I asked someone a question about the work we were doing, even the most genuine collaborative idea was met with her looking at others like, "Why is she here?"

Was this all in my head? Usually I would totally be willing to entertain the idea that my ego was creating an entire one-sided conflict. That is entirely possible, except for the fact that she saved her biggest critique for when I was just out of earshot:

"She's fat and she stinks," she said about me.

So. Yeah. Kind of wished it was just in my head after I heard she'd said that.

Anyway, someone we worked with felt I should know what X said and he told me out of a sense of protectiveness for me. As he talked, his whole face became a wince, as if the words hurt him. I found myself consoling him, as if I had brought this onto him. As if he was the one hurt. The collateral damage of meanness. It was so hard to resist that high school reaction that was welling up inside me, but I kept centered in strong. I'm not going to say it was easy.

"I think she's threatened," my coworker said.

"By what?" I asked.

"By you."

"Uh, no," I said, laughing. Threatened? Like honestly, every fiber of my being was so confused. I decided that when X was around, I was going to maintain my composure, and also be relentlessly kind. You know I wanted to lash out. I wanted to say, "Listen, bitch. You don't know me. You don't know anything about me. How dare you?"

She had said hateful things, so it was easy to cast her as the villain. When I tell people now about the situation, they say, "Well, I would have told her to . . ." No. That was the last thing she needed. Besides, I didn't feel she was worthy of my reaction.

Soon after, a group of us were killing time chatting. The conversation got deep as people shared things about their personal lives. X wasn't saying much, but neither was I. The difference is that I was listening. A coworker confessed that she brought a lot of ideas to work, but worried that she just wasn't good enough to execute them. She felt everyone was better than her. I could completely relate, and I shared what I have learned about comparing myself to other people.

"You know, we all want the same thing," I said, "but we

all go about it in different ways. We all want to be respected and admired, but at the bottom of everything is that we want to be loved."

X broke her silence. "What are you even talking about?"

"You know what I am talking about," I said, looking right at her. "We buy certain things and we wear certain clothes because we want to be admired. Because we want to be loved."

X looked at me like I was judging her, but when she saw from my face that I was coming from an open place, she got quiet.

"Huh," she finally said, more to herself than to us. She is a very intelligent woman, but I don't think she was used to thinking about how badly she was searching for love. And I admit that when I looked at her, I assumed she had been told from a young age that she had worth and value. And then it all clicked for me. She felt inadequate, so she needed me to feel inadequate. Hurt people hurt people.

It made sense, but I admit I still wondered if in X's case, it was really true. And then we had a drinks night for everyone at work.

I guess she'd had a little truth serum by the time I walked into the bar.

"Oh, great," X said as I approached the group. "Here comes Chrissy to steal my thunder."

No one laughed, except me, because this had to be a joke, right? Her words just kind of hung there in the space between us. So I decided to be truthful. I walked up to her and looked her right in the eye with my kindest face.

"I want you to know that no one could ever steal your thunder," I said. "You stand alone in your talent."

X looked at me as if I had two heads. "What?" she said.

"Yeah," I said. "Just so you know."

And what I know is how it feels to feel inadequate and how it feels to be threatened. X and I are very different people, but it doesn't mean we don't have the same echo of insecurities in our behavior. In that moment, I had to be kind. Because when you act the way she acted, and say the things she said, you are clearly upset, hurt, and unkind—but it's not about who you're targeting. Hurting her back would not have solved her problem. She didn't want somebody to be mean back; she wanted acceptance.

I will never believe that it is weakness to "retaliate" with kindness. Our culture has become an arms race of nastiness. I refuse to do it. I don't presume to think that I changed X; only X can change X (now I'm a math teacher). But I do know for sure that if I gave in and let her see me cry or let her see my anger, I would only confirm something for her: my weakness.

Mahatma Gandhi said—why yes, I *am* about to quote Gandhi in reference to dealing with a work beeyotch— "Nobody can hurt me without my permission." Part of being an adult and being emotionally secure is knowing that people's attitudes don't have the power to destroy you. You have the power to decide how to react to the hurt people who want you to feel just as hurt as them.

Nowadays, X has morphed into the trolls waiting for me on social media. *Ooof,* I don't even want you to read the comments about me. Every fat joke known to man, ones that were probably first written in Sanskrit, gets trotted out like it's something new and exciting in nastiness. I could get caught up in them, but then I remember, *Oh, yeah, hurt people hurt people.* Believe me, I want to engage, retaliate, and defend myself because my feelings are hurt. Because it does sting. But the only derogatory thing they can say is that I'm overweight. I am solely being judged on my vessel. Not what's inside, not my loving heart, not my relentless spirit or zest for life. They don't know me. I know me. So I keep it movin'.

And, to paraphrase Gandhi, don't let the beeyotches win.

fourteen

DO WHATCHA WANNA DO

I have always loved expressing myself through fashion, even when I was a kid and there weren't many options for me that were affordable or interesting. There was a store at the mall called Wild Pair that sold funky shoes and socks. For a while, that was my outlet for showing my personality when my clothes weren't that exciting.

When it came time for prom, my group of girlfriends made a pact that we could all go together. Someone decided that we couldn't have the same color dress, so what we were going to wear was everything. I remember thinking, *I'm not gonna find what I actually want on a rack.*

So I asked my mom to make me a dress. I chose a dark purple satin that was within our budget, and she sewed it at night after work. The plan was for it to have capped sleeves and a sweetheart neckline, with an Empire waist and a skirt that sort of flared out. It was going to be the first time any of my classmates ever saw me in a dress.

Four days before prom it was nowhere near done and I was panicking. Then my little sister came home from school with lice and soon gave it to Morgana.

"Mom, if I get lice I can't get my hair done at the salon for prom!" It was going to be the first time that I was having my hair and makeup done for me. My best friend, Kristen, and I were going together and I couldn't miss it.

Thank God, I escaped the lice, but on the day of the prom, my mom was still doing the finishing touches on the dress right up to the last minute. Yet there was something to the frenzy that I loved. It reminded me of the behind-the-scenes footage of fashion shows, when people fuss over the model before sending her out on the catwalk. I thought, *See, I am born for this!*

I think about that when I'm getting ready for an event. You don't know what's going to happen. A button falls off, a sequin comes undone. I have a friend who realized last minute her Spanx were longer than her dress.

YOU RUSH AROUND TO GET TO THESE AWARDS SHOWS, WHICH ARE so much fun but can sometimes feel like the longest weddings you've ever attended. I was at one when a nice-looking woman I didn't know came up to me and told me she loved my dress. She leaned in to give me a hug, so I obliged.

"You know, you should really wear heels," she whispered into my ear.

"Thank you," I said, giving this stranger my sweetest smile. And I thought, *I should really do what I want.*

Look, I appreciate heels, and I think they're wonderful. But I think people are more wonderful. So, if I am going to a fancy event, I don't want to be more concerned about the possibility of breaking my ankle than having a conversation with someone. Besides, I met a stylist who literally had to have a nerve taken out of her foot because of high heels. Heels literally made her lose her nerve, okay?

I know not wearing heels with a fancy dress is such a fashion faux pas, but I am all about comfort first. Because here's the thing: Actors have red-carpet *days* like the Golden Globes—and I know that sounds so pretentious, but hey, dreams come true. So that means eight to ten hours of wearing this outfit. You have to ask yourself, "Am I gonna try to suck in my kidneys and not be able to talk to anybody? Can I even walk in this little number?"

Don't get me wrong, I don't want to go to these events that people put so much work into and look like I didn't care about it or didn't try. I think that's disrespectful. But I have to have options. All women need options. I believe you don't have to compromise fashion just because you want to be comfortable. Or to breathe. Because I think I heard somewhere that that's important to life, right? Breathing.

When I started promoting *This Is Us*, I was worried

about how things would photograph. But I slowly gained confidence. Part of it was learning that I was there to talk about the work of the amazing group of people who are my colleagues, so it wasn't about what I wore. Clothes don't define me. One of the challenges—and it's something I still struggle with—is that voice that urges you to settle. "Oh, it fits. That's fine." I think that's a voice women hear in their head, no matter what the size is on the tag. "This will do." It's harder for me personally, because frankly it is difficult to find things I actually like in my size. I still have the mindset that I am some sort of walking fashion emergency and so as long as I can fit into it, Sold! That's why sometimes I'll be getting dressed for an event and if I don't have the right shoes or the right clutch in the moment, I'll say, "Whatever, who cares?" And then I'll see photographs and think, "Maybe I should have cared."

My reaction to those pictures isn't "Ugh." Instead, my reaction is, "Next time speak your mind, Chrissy."

When magazines wanted to include me, sometimes it felt like the opportunities were brought to me like a miracle. Like the little charity case that could. I am sure there are straight-size women who are excited to get publicity, but the fact that it is such a surprise to a lot of people when I do only makes me more cognizant that plus-size fashion is not really considered fashion yet. Or chic. Or truly acceptable. "Oh, look who snuck in!"

I think the fashion industry is changing when it comes

to plus-size fashion, but it's like everybody is coming off an Ambien. Slowly, and often without much direction. Most urgently, there's my own biggest qualm: the arms. The arms are always so big. Okay, I have a bigger midsection, but that doesn't mean my arms need these yards of silk. Just like in straight sizes, not every plus-size body is shaped the same. Designers must begin to cater to people who are heavier on top or on the bottom, instead of assuming one big size fits all. Because good God, sometimes the tailoring costs me more than the clothes!

In the past few years I've been blessed in so many ways to have a light shining on me. And one of the bonus features of that light is that folks love to pick apart my outfit and fashion choices to make them feel better about themselves. But here's the deal: I love what I've chosen and I feel beautiful every time I take a step onto the red carpet (more on that later). Now, for fun, let's do a full-on *CSI: Red Carpet* on some of my favorite looks.

ALLERGIC TO LATEX

One of my favorite red-carpet looks was the short-sleeved burgundy latex dress I wore to the MTV Movie & TV Awards in 2017. It was custom designed by Jane Doe Latex in Burbank. I had wanted to work with them for a while, and I figured if the Kardashians can do it, why can't I? But listen, I didn't wear it to show that I was interested in latex for, uh, personal enjoyment. It's not that I am not in touch with my sexuality—that just wasn't my statement.

For a long time, I had to beg my stylist to let me wear it.

"Girl, I'm gonna get that," I said.

"Well, if you ever go to some MTV awards show, then we can do it."

When I was nominated for their Next Generation and asked to present, my stylist was my first call.

"Mmmmm, did you check the Internet? I got invited to the MTV awards!" I said. "I'm wearing a latex dress."

So. There are some things you need to be cautious about when wearing a red latex dress. No, not people's reaction. I'll get to that. I'm talking about lubing up to wear it. Also, I had to put down a mat in the car so I wouldn't slide all over the leather seats. Milo Ventimiglia and I got to present the award to Hugh Jackman—who I love—and when he came up to the stage, I whispered to him in a rush of words, "Sir, there's lube on my dress. You probably don't want to hug me."

He gave me the "Girl, are you crazy?" eyes right there in front of everyone.

"It's latex," I whisper-shouted. "Latex."

People got SO hyped about me being in latex. There was a lot of criticism on social media, as if some sort of nasty signal went out. Me in a latex dress literally became news headlines. I had to wonder: *What is it about a big girl in latex that bothers you?* Was it the cut? The waist? My bits weren't showing . . .

I can take criticism about silly stuff in stride, but it bothered me that a lot of the mean comments were couched in a worry that I had been duped into thinking I looked beautiful or cool. They said my stylist had betrayed me, and they wondered if my friends secretly hated me because they didn't tell me how I "really" looked.

I didn't want to strike out at anyone in particular, but I was stung. So, on a whim I tweeted: "For the record, I wear what I want, when I want. News flash it's MY body. #thankstho."

But I wasn't finished. Then I Instagrammed a photo of me in the dress. I didn't comb through a hundred pictures to find the best one; I just grabbed one shot where anyone could look at my face and say, "Oh, that girl is happy." Because I was.

"Remember that time folks got rowdy because I wore a dress?" I captioned the photo. "The outpouring of love and support from all of you lovely people has not gone unnoticed. I hope that in some small way an unconventional body wearing an unconventional material opened up discussion, hearts and minds. I truly had no idea it would make anyone feel uncomfortable, I just wanted to try something different. All I'm saying is do YOU, Boo! Wear what you want, love who you love and treat people the way you want to be treated ♥ Now that that's out of the way, congratulations to all the winners at the @MTV movie and TV awards . . ."

Do *you*, Boo.

LIKE, TOTALLY

If I had a Cinderella moment, it would be when I wore the purple dress to the Golden Globes in January 2017. I had torn the meniscus in my knee from dancing with my ten-year-old nephew at New Year's, but I was determined not to miss my first Globe nomination. (Side note: I needed a wheelchair to get off the plane in LA, starting off a fun set of rumors that I had undergone a gastric bypass. Fun!)

Because of my knee, I wasn't sure I would be able to walk down the red carpet. Like, I honestly asked my team, "What do I do, wheel myself down the carpet? That's a great look." Fortunately, I just needed a knee brace, but I was terrified of having too long a dress or train and that I would get caught up in it. I was so lucky that a designer had been willing to make a couple of dresses for me—but unfortunately, one was just too long and the other just didn't work.

The purple dress I chose, which was a Nathaniel Paul, was originally going to be for another event. I literally woke up out of a deep sleep the night before the Globes, gasping, "I have to wear the purple dress." I called my team when it was a decent hour and told them my decision.

"Oh, thank God," someone said.

"What do you mean, 'Oh, thank God'? You weren't going to tell me you didn't like the other dress?"

But I also understand that they just respected that it had been my choice.

Nathan's dress felt very regal, and yet it wasn't overly fussy, which I loved. Nathan had appeared on *Project Runway*, and he has plus-size women in his family. He gets it, and knows how to flatter a woman without it being too much. People tend to put too much material or bling on a big girl. Like camouflage. We're not trying to hide! Also, he put a jeweled belt—I call it appliqué hardware—at the waist. He wasn't "Let's cover her entire body!" He wanted to accentuate all the positives.

That dress had a lower neckline than I usually wear. It's not like I don't embrace the girls; I just don't want to worry or fuss about "slippage." But the really interesting aspect for me was the bold shoulder design. People expressed their concerns: "You want to look wider?!?" But it worked for me. That powerful statement shoulder made me want to stand up straight and own my space.

There's a radio personality who is a curvy babe, and I like her very much. Well, she had opinions, too, when I went on her show.

"Listen to me, girl," she said to me after she saw me in the dress. "I am a fan of yours; I think you are the bomb, baby. But that dress? What's with the shoulders? You looked like a shower curtain."

"I disagree," I said.

"Your dress looked like it was on a coat hanger," she said.

Well. "Okay, that's cool," I said, "you can have your opinion and it's not going to make me love you any less. That's fine. But I really felt powerful in it."

I really did appreciate her honesty. Everything you do or wear, people are going to have their opinion and that's fine. Just remember that the only opinion that matters is yours. Okuuuur?!

HIPPIE CHIC

It's tricky to find variety with plus-size anything, much less for awards show looks. Like so much in life, you have to create what you want. In January 2017, I decided to design something for the Critics' Choice Awards with my stylist at the time. I had this image of a floor-length floral throwback, and she found this intricate fabric of beautiful embroidered flowers. Being a big girl, you want to hide sometimes, but with that dress, it was like, "Boom! I'm here, in all my embroidered glory."

A lot of people just couldn't get past the fact that a big girl was wearing something that made her stand out. The first thing out of some of the reporters' mouths when they came to interview me was, "Wow, you're wearing a print." So I guess it made a statement, but it was what I wanted to wear. You can't control how it is received or how someone interprets it, but by trusting your instincts and doing what you want, you then educate people about doing the same thing.

FASHION WEEK FITTING (IN)

There I was at Lela Rose's atelier, watching the girls come in to be fitted for fashion week. I was about eighteen sizes larger than the models. Yet people were putting just as much care into making sure that my Emmy dress was right for me and that I was happy with how I looked. I didn't feel better than or less than; I just felt equal to a girl who, I'm certain, must have been a double zero. I never felt embarrassed or worried. We were in this together, both seeing what worked best for us. It was this amazing moment for me, in that I was reminded that it doesn't matter what size you are, it's how you feel about yourself. Confidence, like beauty, is an inside job.

Innately I had that confidence because of who I am as a person, and how I want to be treated and how I want to treat people. But I had never been in this situation, in someone's atelier where they are designing clothes for fashion week. Maybe it felt right because I had spent years putting little deposits in my self-confidence bank.

Lela's team had created a sketch for me to visualize the details of my dress. There were two color choices, and I picked what I later coined "deep sea green." I wanted it to be dramatic to honor the night, but a girl needs a back-story. It was a dark color, but I wanted to stand out. It was embellished with two rows of pearls and complemented by crystals all over the bottom. What a gift to have such a gown made for my first Emmy nomination!

JOY & PAIN

I was going to the NAACP Image Awards, and I wanted to honor the night by making a visual statement about be-ing present and standing in your space. Michael Costello was kind enough to create a fun, bubblegum-fuchsia num-ber made just for me. (It serves no one if the instinct is to say, "Oh don't make this dress for me, I don't deserve it." Instead, I want to be someone who says, "Thank you. I am going to wear it with joy and pride.")

This dress was the ultimate answer to anyone who thinks plus-size people should stick to black. My mom was visiting me in Los Angeles during this time, and she came with me for the fitting.

"This is just a fitting, right?" she said. "You're not wear-ing that dress."

"Uh, yeah, Mom," I said. "It's a check-fit. This is what I'm wearing tonight."

"Oh."

"Mom, why did you have to say that right now?" Just

saying that was big for me. I normally don't talk to my mother this way, but it hurt so much that I had to say that in a roomful of people. The hardest part was that I knew her comment came from a good place.

"I just don't think it's flattering."

"Okay, well, thank you for sharing that with me."

But sometimes it's not about it being flattering. It's about the color or the shape or the design. That dress was about celebrating living by my own rules. And I loved it.

So yeah, everyone is going to have an opinion. Even your own mother.

BECAUSE I GET TO WEAR PRETTY DRESSES A LOT NOW, I OFTEN GET asked if I have any rules about fashion. My rule is to break all of them. First of all, why do we have them? We have rules and laws to protect people. Who are we protecting with fashion rules? Because I don't think those laws are there to protect *me*. Who am I gonna hurt with a dress? You and I know the Fashion Police aren't doling out tickets on the streets of Hollywood because folks are in actual danger of coming to terms with their prejudices. As a plus-size woman, I'm typically the usual suspect. *Bloop-bloop!*

wear what makes you happy

So let's take a look at the rules and regulations for dressing while plus-size. Don't show your arms. No body contouring. In fact, you're not allowed to wear anything tight at all. You would never want to show any folds, curves, inconsistencies, or, God forbid, your tummy. Never wear anything too revealing. You can't be sexy if you're a plus-size woman. Your skirt can't be too short, and we just want to make sure you understand what we said about tight clothes being a big no. In fact, wear black from head to toe, stay silent, and please just let everyone forget you exist. Cool?

You are pretty much told to cover up because your body is offensive to the world. We are so trained in these fashion rules that plus-size women internalize them. We police ourselves and do our best not to cause "trouble" by even being seen. These rules are so ingrained in us, we begin to think they're for our own good. But they come from people who feel uncomfortable when they see images of plus-size women.

Does the discomfort come from "Oh, they're unhealthy and that makes me feel a certain way"? Or is it—plot twist— "Hmmm, I think I am attracted to this person. What does that mean about me? Who am I?"

Again, what people think about you is none of your business. You do what makes you happy, and you can't control how it makes other people feel. It's your life. Why would you live for anybody else? The whole point of us being here is to be ourselves.

I have my own tips to share with you, but I don't want you to think of them as rules. These are just the things it took me a while to figure out about getting dressed, and I want to save you some time so you get to the party faster.

1. WEAR WHATEVER THE HELL YOU WANT.

There, I said it. Peer pressure can be tricky when you're growing up. Even positive messages like "That looks really great on you" or helpful advice about accentuating different parts of your body can make you feel like you're dressing to please someone else. I don't care if a stylist says something is perfect; if I don't want to wear it, I don't want to wear it.

Recently, there was a dress that was custom made for me. I thought, *This is just not for me.* I might be thirty-seven but I don't want to dress matronly, no matter how pretty everyone else thought the dress was. Whereas one person said it was vintage, to me it just felt dated. And I spoke up for myself: "I'm just not interested in wearing it. I just don't like it."

2. PUT THE SCRIPT DOWN.

In TV and film, we have these things called loglines, which are one-sentence summaries of whatever project you're working on. When *This Is Us* was a pilot, the logline was "Dramedy follows an ensemble—some of them sharing the same birthday—whose life stories intertwine in curious ways." There are people who can put a logline on their fashion: "Classic cuts with modern fabrics." Or "The everyday couture." But I wake up and some days want to wear something different. Color blocking one day, a little retro the next. Or even just making it simple comfort—it doesn't always have to be about dressing to the nines.

Wear what feels good when you put it on in that moment.

3. THINK OUTSIDE THE BOX.

I've been so inspired and educated by all sorts of folks, women of every size and shape and on every platform. "Ooooh, I could wear this! Or I could wear that. Why don't

I try this?" If you see them take risks, let that encourage you to take risks yourself. Don't be afraid.

4. LET IT GO.

One babe's trash might be another babe's treasure. Give away the pieces you no longer wear or fit into, or that dress that looked great on the rack but fit terribly at home. Get rid of them, and don't let them clutter up your closet and your mind. They'll get over it, I promise. If the clothes are businessy, donate them to an organization like Dress for Success. They have helped nearly one million (!) women try to achieve economic independence. I just did an event for them, and they help women who are dealing with life changes, whether they have lost a job or are going through a divorce. Whatever their situation, when they are ready to get back in the workforce they can go and feel like a woman, as opposed to getting a handout. The organization also has programs that help women with interviewing and budgeting.

At the event, I spoke to one of the Dress for Success ambassadors. She told me, "I came in for a pair of shoes and my life was completely changed." She has savings for her family now. I thought about my mom, who had four children on her own before marrying Trigger. I can't imagine what it would have done for her to have that support to go on job interviews so she could provide for her family. There are so many people who don't have the resources or who have been through a traumatic experience that leaves them not knowing which way is up.

And don't forget: there's also Career Gear, which provides men with business and business-casual clothes to land interviews.

5. MAKE A GREAT TAILOR YOUR BESTIE.

No article of clothing is one-size-fits-all. And you are worth going to the tailor to get the fit that you want. A good fit can change your life.

6. HONOR THE OCCASION.

A lot of people get timid about dressing up because they are afraid of looking like they're trying too hard. But turn that idea around. If someone comes to your birthday party and is dressed up, do you think, "Who does she think she is?" No, you think, "Aww, she cared about this event. She cares about me." So, show people you care about them. The same is true of your job. Remember that old adage: "Dress for the job you want, not the job you have."

7. CONFIDENCE IS THE BEST ACCESSORY.

For better or for worse, when someone looks you up and down, that person is getting a whole message—one that has nothing to do with the number on the tag or what you paid for your outfit. The first thing the person will see is your confidence. Because you could wear the most expensive dress, but if you don't feel good mentally or emotionally, it doesn't matter what you're wearing.

8. PEOPLE WILL BE CHALLENGED BY
THAT CONFIDENCE.

Sometimes people get jealous when they see you own your look, no matter how humbly you go about it. There will be a smaller-size girl who looks amazing in a particular outfit but just doesn't feel comfortable. Meanwhile, there's a girl who is a size 22 who is just, like, killing the game. People might feel a need to bring her down. One of the secret weapons people use is "I wish I had your confidence." I am perplexed by this statement and I initially took offense at it. We all know what they're really saying: "How can you feel this good but look so bad?" Well, my friends, there's a complicated response, but I will give you the CliffsNotes: If you can't love yourself for who you are right now, you'll never get to the place you're meant to be.

9. CHANNEL YOUR INNER ROCK STAR.

I don't want to just fit in. Why fit in when you're supposed to stand out, right? If you start to feel down about not being able to just grab something off the rack—whether it's because of the size or the price—think about all those amazing musicians who take the stage in clothes that are singularly theirs. Whether it's a $1.50 T-shirt from Goodwill or a dress you had to have tweaked by a tailor, embrace the notion that your look is one of a kind. Because you are one of a kind.

fifteen

RETURN ON
THE INVESTMENT

Dear All,

I first want to thank you for this amazing opportunity. Last night felt like Christmas Eve! While I've never dreamed of sugarplums, believe it or not, I have always wished for a role like this. I was so moved by this character, that I've asked my agent to pass this letter on to you all.

Aside from the obvious physical aspects of Kate, this is my life. I am KATE. I have been the second fiddle, assistant and the sidekick to many successful people. All the while, questioning why I am so close yet so far away. I have been so broken that I have almost given it all up.

While my weight has been a steady struggle both in business and my personal life, it has also been a beautiful up hill battle of self-discovery.
I have been gifted to teach tolerance and share my journey with women and men who know all too well of discrimination for their size but desperately want to change. I want to be a visible inspiration to all who pursue their dreams and especially for those who think they lack a fighting chance.

I have lost over 100lbs on my own. I am committed to Kate's evolution and I would be honored to embody your vision of her.

While I know there are other wonderful ladies in the running, I had to express my unwavering love for this incredible life-changing role. From the moment my agent sent me the breakdown, to the first time I read the script, I have never felt like a role was written more for me. This story is so heartwarming and charming. It just rings so true to me, that I can't imagine someone else bringing it to life. I embody and walk "Kate's" life every single day, and I am hoping that you will see that too. It is the air I breathe and I want to be able to bring that to life for you.

Regardless of what happens, I cannot thank you enough from the bottom of my mushy heart for this awesome experience. It has been a life changing moment for me.

Warmest Regards,

Chrissy Metz
Chrissy Metz

I wrote this letter after I did the first of two screen tests for *This Is Us*. I wanted Dan Fogelman, the creator of the show, to know that I appreciated that he was telling the story of a woman who was truly dealing with her weight. Not in the "Oh my God, I gained a pound from my stressful job" way. With Kate Pearson, he had created a woman who was really struggling. She wasn't a caricature or the butt of the joke. She was living in the shadow of her brother and had gone to LA but was stuck, not knowing what she wanted to do with her life. And she was dealing with a lack of confidence stemming from her weight issues.

The first time I read her lines in the script, all I could think of was *Oh my God, I am Kate*. And then, *I have to be on this show. Please.*

Back then the script was called "Untitled Dan Fogelman Project: A Pilot." As the script went around, everyone wanted to be a part of it. I had just one problem: I needed new head shots. Head shots cost money, it turns out, and I didn't have any. At the time, I was working back in the office, transitioning my clients to their new agent and making sure they were all taken care of. My plan was to audition full-time so I could get out of it. Whereas the agency used to cover my cell phone bill and car payments, that had stopped. My friend Gina had taken me in, letting me stay at her place and contribute what I could for the rent. I really wanted to get my shots done by Dana Patrick, who is an amazing photographer, so I needed to figure out how to get nine hundred dollars. I didn't want to ask any friends to lend me money and I couldn't ask my family, so I decided to take out a payday loan. I had to trust that I could pay it all back at once.

When I got the head shots, my agent sent them in, pitching me on the strength of my recent credit with *American Horror Story.* It showed a bit of experience to get me in the door, instead of "Oh, there's this girl who says she's really like this character."

Thank God I got an audition. The casting director was working out of the Sony lot, and as I drove over there, the morning just seemed different. The skies were bluer; the birds were birdier. I felt like Belle in *Beauty and the Beast,* walking through her little village.

"Good morning!" said the security guard.

"Good morning!" I singsonged. Everything was in Technicolor, and I don't know if it was because I wanted the role so badly or I knew I had lived this and could bring something real to it. There was magic in the air.

And then.

I walked in the door and saw a couple of the same girls I see at auditions. *Whomp-whomp-whomp.*

The audition scene was the one where Kate has just fallen off her scale and her brother Kevin has come to help. I sat in the chair, propping up my right leg. The casting director had me do the scene, and in the back of my mind I was thinking, *Oh God, this is the worst audition I have ever had in my life.*

"Okay, thanks," she said.

"You're welcome!" I said.

"Thanks for coming in," she said.

Sigh. "You're welcome."

You know when something is so close you can taste it? And then it's snatched right out of your mouth? Yeah. But the thing about auditioning is that sometimes they see something in you that you can't. They can see that there is some innate part of you that is right for whatever it is you are trying to achieve; you just need to get there.

There was something there in me, because they brought me in for a callback, this time auditioning for Dan Fogelman, and John Requa and Glenn Ficarra. I got another call, this time to do a screen test. They had one request: "We need you to dye your hair darker."

My hair was red with blond highlights at the time, kind of like my mom's.

"Okay," I said. Oh man, I wouldn't be able to use those head shots anymore!

They had the characters of Kevin and Kate down to five guys and five girls, and we were all brought in for the test. This was the first time I met Justin Hartley, and I read with him once. It felt right. We were clicking. The best part is that he is obviously super-gorgeous, but I am not into blonds. I crush a lot, but man, it would be weird to have a crush on the guy playing your brother. It also has to be said again and again that his looks are secondary to all that makes him wonderful. He is so talented and thoughtful and funny.

Obviously, everyone agreed, because he was already cast when I was brought in for a second screen test. It had come down to me and another actress, who is funny, smart, and beautiful. NBC wanted to test us both with Justin.

There was just one issue: I had eighty-one cents in my bank account. I was freaking out because I wasn't sure if I had enough gas in my car to get to NBC Universal. And you needed to have at least twenty dollars in your bank account to swipe your card at the gas pump.

Thank God I made it there, and as soon as I walked in I saw the girl up against me. She looked more like Justin, and I was certain she was going to get the part.

"It's your job," I said.

"No, it's your job," she said back.

"Well, whoever's it is," I said, "God bless us both."

After we both tested, Justin walked out with us to the parking structure. He said goodbye, and it felt very awkward because I was either going to go on this journey with him as his sister or I was going to go home and not be a Pearson.

I got into my car, and as I was about to call my agent, a number I didn't know showed up on my cell. I assumed it was a bill collector, so I ignored it. The girl with eighty-one cents can't help you.

As I drove out of my space and through the maze of the parking structure, I called my agent.

"It went terribly," I told him. "I'm not gonna get the job." It hadn't, but I didn't want him to have any illusions. I just felt they were going to go with the other actress.

"I'm sure—fine, Chriss—" He was cutting up. I couldn't even make a call right because I was losing service driving around this parking structure. Then I heard a *BEEP*, and it was that freaking number calling again.

"Let me see who this is," I said. I switched over, and what I heard was like "Mxyzptlk."

"HELLO?" I yelled.

I could make out "—y."

"This is *Chrissy*. CHRISSY."

"We know who we called," said the voice as I made yet another turn.

"Oh. Right."

"This is Da—Foge—n."

Oh, Dan Fogelman! I thought, *This could be really bad, or this could be really good.*

"Hi, so we just wanted to let you know—" The phone cut off again.

Oh God, oh God. Know *what?*

"I'm sorry?"

"We just wanted to tell you that you're our girl."

"WHAAAAAAT?" I screamed, "Are you kidding me?"

"No!" he said.

I realized I hadn't been paying attention to the road. "I don't even know where I'm going," I told Dan. "I think I'm going out the entrance."

"No!" he said. "Don't. We need you!"

In my home, I have a framed copy of an email sent to Dan Fogelman from his producing partner Jess Rosenthal. The chain starts with "Just curious, who got Kate?"

"Chrissy," writes Dan.

"Yeeeesssss!!!!" is Jess's reply.

When the first episode premiered, Dan framed the email and sent it to my house. He is literally the kindest, most humble human being that you will ever meet. It's absurd how giving he is. Dan Fogelman is solely responsible for changing my life. He wrote a role for someone we'd never seen before.

"It's always going to be about the weight for me," Kate says in a monologue in the second episode. "That's been my story ever since I was a little girl. And every moment that I'm not thinking about it, I'm thinking about it. Like, will this chair hold me? Will this dress fit me? And if I ever get pregnant, will anyone ever notice? It's just at the core of who I am, it's just deep inside, and eight tequila shots can only mask that for a couple hours."

I remember reading those lines and running to Dan, saying, "These are my fears." And I love that now, Kate is evolving to a place where that is not her only storyline. That was just the beginning of her story.

When we meet Kate, she is weighing herself half-naked on the scale. I had to find comfort in that discomfort and use it for the scene. It was important for Kate and the journey she is going on, and for me, and also for the women in hair and makeup who gasped and told me they could never do that. It's a comment on how we are judged for the way we look and a feeling everyone can relate to. I take off my earrings, because Kate's in a place where she feels every ounce counts. Reese Witherspoon told me when I met her, "We've all done it." People of all walks of life respond to Kate, because we *all* feel vulnerable. We have all gotten caught up in our inadequacies, but if we move through them, we can learn and get where we want to be. And time and again, I have seen that the answer to what we really want, the reason people connect to Kate, is that wish to love and be loved.

AS CLOSE AS THE CAST IS NOW, WE DIDN'T ALL GET TOGETHER UNTIL the table read. Well, we all squeezed into the little kitchen at the NBC Universal lot first. There was Mandy Moore and Milo Ventimiglia as Mom and Dad Pearson, and Sterling K. Brown and Justin Hartley as brothers Randall and Kevin. We talked about karaoke and movies we'd seen, Sterling getting the conversations going.

Then we sat at one big conference room table with assigned seats. I sat between Justin and Chris Sullivan, the actor who plays Kate's fiancé, Toby.

It's hard to believe now that I had never met Chris before the table read. I feel like he has always been there supporting me. I didn't test with him, and in fact I tested with other actors auditioning for the role. But when we met, I just knew *Oh, yeah, this is gonna be good.* And it's been amazing ever since. Watch him onscreen and you know what I go through trying to keep a straight face. His nuances and choices as an actor are incredible, and he can show so much in one look or a fist-bump. For me to play the straight guy to the funnyman is so difficult, since I like to make people laugh so much. I can't tell you how many times I have thought to myself, *I'm gonna ruin this take. I'm gonna ruin this take. Okay, Chrissy. You can do this. You don't have to . . .* But with him as my partner, I make it through.

And from the beginning, Chris gave me courage. He helped me with my lines because I was too afraid to memorize them. I was frozen, because there was a chance of failure if I actually moved forward.

"Chris, I don't know my line," I said. This was the second episode, when we are sitting on the edge of the wall at the Hollywood party we go to with Kevin.

"Yeah you do."

"Chris, what is it?"

He told me. And I did know it, but he was so kind and didn't make me feel like an idiot. He looked me right in the eye and said, "You've got this." He could have sabotaged me. There are actors who do that—nobody on our set, but they are out there.

I have enough concerns about sabotaging myself. That early belief that I didn't know my lines was just my fear of success. I worried about making the right choices on how I wanted to deliver the lines. I was showing up for myself, and I hadn't done that a lot. To do my work now, I had to do that a hundred times a day for every line, for every scene, for every other person.

It is very easy to feel outclassed on our set, no matter how much I love each amazing person. Sterling is so good it is distracting. I don't have many scenes with him, but I will watch him and get so caught up that I forget I need to get ready for my own scene. He has the most contagious laugh, and sometimes he'll laugh so hard he will fall to his knees or onto his back. It is such pure joy that I can't help but want to involve myself in his laughter. I watch him and our Beth, Susan Kelechi Watson, and I'm just like, *Give them all the awards. All of 'em.* Susan is so subtle and brilliant in her acting that people think she *is* Beth. She is so much fun, loves karaoke, and she is funny as . . . heck.

And when I start to feel like the new kid in school again, worrying that I'm not as experienced as the other actors, there's Sterling calling out of the blue with encouragement.

"Sister," he always says.

"Brother," I always answer.

"You're killing the game."

"Stop!"

"Do you know I love you, Chrissy Metz?"

"What?"

"I just love you."

"Oh Sterling, you don't know how much I needed to hear that."

We're all there for each other that way. Mandy and Milo have also looked out for us—like they have this amazing parenting energy that extends to real life. I'm not sure if it's the longevity of their careers that gives them the confidence to extend that to us, but I'll take it. I'm older than Mandy, but I believe she is way more mature than me. And Milo, oh, Milo—from the beginning, he was the captain of the ship. He is always asking me, "You holding up? You need anything, Chris?" He's the only person in my life besides my grandmother who has called me Chris, and I embrace it and love it.

Even on photo shoots he will sort of take the reins. When we did our first ever photo shoot as a cast for the show, it was when the title being kicked around was *Happy Birthday*. The art director had brought in birthday hats for us to wear to create a zany look.

"Yeah, we're not putting on the birthday hats," Milo said from the jump. It wasn't tough or nasty, it was just sure. At that point, I felt so new that I am sure I would have done whatever was asked. Instead, I agreed: "Yeah, what he said."

On the set, Milo is the guy who is looking out for everyone. His thing is that he always has a handkerchief in his back pocket to give you if you are crying or sweating under the lights. He's *that* guy.

One day we were doing a Q&A and I was crying because, well, that's what I do.

"Oh my God, Milo," I said. "I'll get your handkerchief dry-cleaned."

"You're good," he said, taking it back from me.

"You just took back your dirty handkerchief."

"Don't worry about it."

When we are in a group and a fan sees us, it can be overwhelming for that person. One time Justin, Milo, Chris, and I were in Utah at a charity event. This woman came up to us and couldn't speak. She didn't even know where to look, she was so emotional.

"Okay," Milo said to the woman, putting his hand lightly on her arm to calm her. "What's your name?"

"Uh, uh . . ."

"What's your name?"

It was something like Samantha.

"Okay, Samantha. Yes, we can take a picture." He took the phone from her and perfectly set up a selfie with her and all of us. He is Jack Pearson in real life, y'all.

And Mandy is totally a mothering force. There are some times when the Pearson family gets together on set during a break and she is in the old-age makeup. She is incredibly professional and doesn't break character one bit. It's so commendable, and I think, *Oh, no wonder she's wildly successful.*

People ask me, "Is she real?" and I say, "Oh, Mandy is real." She is such a beautiful human being, and she is genuinely a good person. She is so thoughtful that she tricked me for Christmas last year. Our costumer came up to me on set and asked me all casually, "Chrissy, what kind of metal do you like for jewelry? White gold, silver, rose gold . . . ?"

I thought it was for Kate's engagement ring from Toby.

"I have a choice?" I asked. "Wow, I love rose gold."

"Okay," she said. "Let's just make sure about the size of the ring."

Cut to four months later. For Christmas, Mandy presented me a beautiful ring she had made for me with my initials. In rose gold.

She ran a four-month con just to be that thoughtful! "Mandy *Moore*!" I yelled. "I can't take it."

I WOULD SAY 98 PERCENT OF THE TIME, I AM CONFIDENT AND SE-cure. Oh, but that 2 percent. The *This Is Us* cast is so smart and well-spoken that when we do group interviews, I worry that my spontaneity is actually me putting my foot in my mouth.

I don't think anyone will mind if I tell you that we all have a secret text chain that we share jokes and GIFs on. The chain includes Mandy, Milo, Sterling, Justin, Chris,

Susan, Ron, Dan, and Glenn. Everybody is so clever, and at times I get those nerves again, that feeling of "I'm not smart enough to respond." But I can't *not* respond, because then I'll look like a jerk, or like I am too busy to respond and I'm not prioritizing these relationships. So I say to myself, *Chrissy, stop. You are perfectly made. Sterling is also perfectly made, and Mandy and Milo and everyone else. I am the way I am.*

When that 2 percent of me takes over for a second, I wonder if everyone else feels the way I get, sometimes. The answer, I've learned from talking to so many people about what the show does for them, is yes. We beat ourselves up. And sometimes, we all just have to fake it until we make it.

When have I faked it to make it? Oh, last week on set. John and Glenn, the duo who directed the pilot, were back to direct an episode. They are awesome, but I went to set saying, "I so don't know if I can do this."

We were filming a scene where I was on the phone. I was not in the scene with anybody, and those are really challenging for me because I have to rely solely on myself, my ability, and being present. And that is hard, because I haven't always shown up for myself.

During the filming, I got hot and I started sweating, which is what I do when I am nervous. And I of course thought I was profusely sweating, which only made me more anxious.

Also, I had to be doing "business"—which is what actors call doing things in a scene while acting; in this case, cooking. Doing "business" makes me uncomfortable because I never want to look unrealistic or inauthentic. I had to cut up food in the kitchen, answer a cell phone, and hit a mark. And the whole time I was preparing, I was thinking, *Do I really deserve to be here? Maybe there is someone better for this job.*

I was trying to talk myself out of what I was supposed to do that day and I caught myself. "Chrissy," I said aloud. "Just do the damn scene."

In that scene, and in life, sometimes you have to do what you have to do and not worry about being perfect. The real secret is to focus on the bigger picture. Not just yourself. Think about it: My ego was telling me that everything rode on me hitting my mark and nailing my line. But what about the directors? What about the crew? There were thirty people making sure the lighting was right and there were thousands of dollars on the line for that scene alone. Wait, it's not about me at all. We're a team.

When we, again, l'eggo our ego, we can come back to that place of humility and say: Do the work, be prepared, show up for yourself, *and* show up for everyone else.

I got through the scene and, guess what? I didn't die.

But there will always be those moments when I become frightened that something is too hard. When I want to stall and say, "I have to go to the bathroom. I have to change my shoes." Or whatever. When that happens to you, let it go. Do your best and keep it moving. Every day.

WHEN I SAW THE SCRIPT FOR THE THIRD EPISODE OF *THIS IS US*, I quickly scanned it and saw there was a scene with Kate where her lines were in italics.

"*Lying in my bed, I hear the clock tick and think of you.*"

That meant she was singing. Wait. Kate's singing? Kate's singing "Time After Time"?

I ran to Dan and attempted to be very subtle about my excitement. "DAN!" I screamed.

He knew exactly what was up. "Don't worry if you can't sing," he said. "We'll just get someone to dub it."

"No, Dan, I want to try!"

"Really?"

I never sang in my auditions, and Dan had no idea how important music is to me. He couldn't have known how much I wanted to sing "Doll Parts" on *American Horror Story*. Now I was going to sing as Kate!

We shot the scene at an old folks' home, which was so crazy because when I studied with my vocal coach Dot, she used to have us sing at retirement facilities over the holidays. This time, there were thirty background artists who were either half-asleep in real life or making an acting choice to be asleep. I looked around and thought, *Oh, they are not interested in what I have to sing.*

But I had to give a performance, and I didn't have a choir to hide in, or a band to blend in with. They miked me, and Glenn and John recorded me for the show. What you heard on the show was me recording it live, so they could capture the most authentic sound.

"Wait a minute," I said when they started rolling. "Y'all didn't tell me that was the plan."

It meant a lot to me, because singing was my first love and what I have always wanted to do. But, like Kate, I was really afraid and never supported or encouraged in that. Luckily they made it more of a storyline, incorporating it into Kate's always wanting to be like her mom.

That first scene where I sang worked because I used my nerves. I started off tiny and a bit shaky, and eventually got comfortable, just as Kate would. Here's an actor secret—we just use what's happening. That's the only thing you can do because the more you resist, the more the fear persists. Whatever you're feeling, lean in and use it.

I like to say lean into love, but I know sometimes fear and vulnerability are the most pressing emotions we have. I spent so many years resisting a feeling of vulnerability, and now it is exactly what allows me to do what I love most, which is to connect with people.

the power of an apology

At the end of my first day of being on the *This Is Us* set, I drove myself out of the Fox lot. I was exhausted from spending the day shooting a treadmill scene. When you first get on the lot, they give you a little scan ticket, and when you leave, you have to give it back for security purposes.

I was in another world, so I missed the bucket you're supposed to drop it in from your car and tried to just drive through. And the security guard wouldn't lift the gate.

"Do you have your scan ticket?" he asked me in an annoyed tone.

"Yeah," I answered, bringing him all the exhaustion I was carrying and laying it at his feet.

"Well, why didn't you put it in the bucket?"

"Well, I didn't *see* the bucket."

"There's clearly a sign," he said.

"Well, I didn't see it," I said. We were just trying to battle each other. "Are you not going to me let me out now? I've already passed it. Do you want the ticket?"

"Just . . . here," he said, lifting the gate for me.

The second I was driving on the road I thought, *I want to eat something.* I wanted a cheeseburger. A cookie. Clearly, in my life I have often chosen not to share my emotions and instead eat about them. This works for a second to numb those feelings. It fills the void and helps you not to deal with what's really going on.

But this time I stopped myself. "Hold on, hold on, Chrissy," I said aloud. "Why did you treat that man this way? Why didn't you say, 'Would you mind throwing it in the bucket for me?' Or what about asking for advice, like 'What should I do?' What a concept."

That's what it was about. I was embarrassed about not knowing what to do. I decided I wasn't going to go home without making things right. So I turned the car right around and drove back onto the lot. I can't imagine what that guard thought when Miss Ticketude rolled back to his gate.

"Hi, I'm the brat," I said. "Also known as Chrissy. You challenged me and I reacted. I was wrong. I didn't see the sign and I should have just said that."

"What?" he said.

There was another guard in the booth with him, who

started laughing. "Are you coming here to apologize?" the other guard said. And then he paused. "Wow."

My guy nodded.

"So, I'm really sorry for being a bitch," I said. "It was my fault."

"I can't believe you came back to say you're sorry," said my guy, who was now firmly *my* guy.

"Me either," I said. "So. Anyway. I hope to see you again. Have a great night."

"Goodbye," my new friends said together.

We often snap back or lash out because our egos are hurt. We often won't do things like apologize because our egos won't let us. If I hadn't gone back, I would still be reeling about it all night. And, more likely, I would have eaten about it. Which wouldn't have worked, because I would have continued to be upset and pissed off. For what? Because I didn't see a sign and couldn't admit to it? That's crazy making.

And every single time I left that lot I would have remembered that mistake. I would stew, and I would imagine the guard hated me. Then I would resent him for hating me for a simple mistake. Instead, I freed myself. And I hope I freed him, too.

sixteen

A REASON, A SEASON, OR A LIFETIME

Forgiveness. Lawd.

A lot of people love the father-daughter relationship I have with Milo Ventimiglia on the show. As you know, I didn't have that in my own life. When I got to Los Angeles, I didn't even want to use Metz as my last name. I didn't want my biological father, Mark, to get any credit whatsoever for my success when and if it did come. He didn't want any part of us when he divorced my mom and abandoned us in poverty, so why should I carry his name?

Then I got famous. And he wanted back in. It started with Facebook posts and shout-outs, and I thought, *okay, maybe we can start to be cordial.* But as soon as I extended the olive branch, it seemed as if he wanted the tree.

"How much money are you making on that show?"

Those are the first words Mark said to me after twenty years of nothing.

He is sixty-six now, and on his fourth wife. I was in his house because of my older sister, Monica, who lives twenty minutes from him and had been trying to create a relationship with our dad. I was in Florida for Christmas and I went with Monica to exchange Christmas gifts and have dinner. I didn't give him an answer. The look in his eye was clear: "How much are you worth now?" The answer is that I am worth just as much now as I was when he decided I was worthless at eight years old.

I'd brought him a lot of food from a health food store that day. He'd previously had health issues and was attempting to lose weight per doctor's orders, so I was trying to be thoughtful.

"Thank you," he said.

"You're welcome," I said.

"I don't have anything for you."

"That's fine."

"I didn't know you were coming," he said.

"I'm just here to see you."

I felt a softening, but only slightly. As a grown-up, I know that I don't understand what happened in his childhood that made him act the way he did as an adult. There's a reason he did what he did, and I don't know what that is. What I can do is look at the lesson about how not to be.

Otherwise, I don't get anything good from dwelling on it. If it's not helpful, it's hurtful, right?

That day he acted as if twenty years hadn't passed, and we were the closest friends. It was almost delusional. I'd extended the olive branch by coming to visit, but his response was too much. Mark is a stranger to me and I had absolutely no idea how to magically bridge the gulf between us.

Then he asked me again, "How much are you making on that show?"

I sort of laughed it off and said, "It's none of your business."

I immediately felt foolish, and I felt like I was betraying my mother. When she found out that I was going to see Mark, she said. "Oh, now he wants to show up?"

The following February, I was on *Entertainment Tonight* and Kevin Frazier asked me about my relationship with my father, and I was honest. "There is still a lot of resentment in the family," I explained, "toward him for leaving us."

I guess Mark's friends told him about that interview, because the story he had been telling about his involvement in my life did not match mine. I think he was thoroughly embarrassed. He called Monica, demanding to come to her house. "I can't believe Chrissy threw me under the bus!" he yelled.

And wonderful Monica, my courageous big sister, had my back. "What makes you think she wants to have a relationship with you when the first thing you ask her is about money?" she asked. "What about all the trauma you put us through as kids?"

"What are you talking about?"

"We know what you put Mom through. The cheating—"

"What, what—*what*?" he yelled. "Who told you that?"

"You're gonna sit in my house and lie to me?" said Monica. "If you keep lying to me then you can take your fat ass right out of my house. You had a relationship with Phillip. He was your everything. You had a relationship with me. But you had no relationship with Chrissy."

"Well, your mother—"

"Don't blame my mother for anything. You know how to pick up a phone. You know how to write a letter. You're not blaming my mother for anything. Because all my mom—all *our* mother—did was support us and make sure that we had a roof over our heads, while you're on your fourth marriage and not giving a shit about anyone else."

"I'm not gonna take this."

"Well, you can just sit here and take the truth. And you need to handle it if you want to be in her life."

Sigh. My sister is my hero.

EARLIER THIS MONTH, JUST AFTER THANKSGIVING, MY LITTLE SISTER Morgana gave me a call. Someone saying she was a journalist had stopped by her house way out in the country. Morgana's husband offered to take the woman's name and number, saying, "If she wants to get in touch with you she will."

She didn't, and Morgana immediately called Trigger to warn him something was up.

"Oh yeah," he said. "She already came by to talk to me. I let her in the house and she took pictures."

The woman stopped at Monica's house, too, but she didn't answer the door. We learned what was up when the *Daily Mail* posted a long interview with Trigger and my stepsister, Rebecca, alongside photos of them posed at my childhood home. In it, Trigger talks at length about my weight, then says, "We never put any pressure on her to eat differently or work out."

Whaaat? I just didn't know what to do with that. He thinks that he said I could eat whatever I wanted, and yet he weighed me constantly? Wow. Okay. But I had to believe that he was just taken advantage of. Besides, I know the truth.

The very next day, Morgana was at the grocery store when she saw a headline in the *National Enquirer*. She sent me a screenshot, and I guess it was Mark's turn with the reporter. Above a picture of my biological father, Mark, a headline screamed:

CHRISSY ABANDONED *ME*

NAVYMAN METZ BLAMES EX FOR SHATTERING FAMILY. *THIS IS US* STAR'S DAD TELLS ALL

In the article, which the *Enquirer* called a "blockbuster," he insists I've shut him out and calls my mom a liar. Somehow, his eight-year-old daughter abandoned him. Or maybe as an adult, as a father, he couldn't take responsibility for his actions.

I'd only skimmed Trigger's article, but I read every word of this one. Because let's face it: I would like to have a relationship with a father figure—one who is my actual father. But reading the article, where he talks about all the times he reached out, I had to wonder what his real intention was. Because if he really wanted to have a genuine relationship, why was this retaliation against me in a national tabloid more important than having a conversation with me?

It would be so different if he had said, "You know, I was absent. I am sorry. I want to make it up to you." But we can't write lines for people just because we want to hear them. He never once said he was sorry, because he obviously doesn't feel like he did anything wrong. And that bothers me. How do you forgive someone for something when he refuses to acknowledge that he has done anything to forgive?

I have sat with that question while sharing my stories with you, and the best answer I have is that I guess you have to forgive the person for yourself. For your own sanity. I have come to terms with my dad being who he is. And if he doesn't want to change, that's okay. If he doesn't want to even see the other side of the coin, that's okay, too. My ego wants to say, "You're wrong. You're a liar. Let me tell you about your ass." But for what? What will that solve? If he's shown me who he is time and time again, and that never serves but in fact hurts me, I don't have to be in a relationship with him.

I can meet him where he is, but I can move forward.

give back to others (and to yourself)

I was being interviewed on the Golden Globes red carpet when she stopped to say hello. The power and the glory that is Niecy Nash in a gorgeous red dress. Now, I have been a fan of hers ever since she was on *Clean House*, her home makeover show. Let's face it, I didn't care about the house—I cared about every funny thing that beautiful woman said.

Of course I just had to tell her.

"And baby!" she said, barely letting me finish gushing. "I want to be friends with you. Girl, I've been watching your show. You are fire."

What do you say but yes? She is one of those people who light up a room in such a humble way and just want to include others.

We exchanged numbers. "I'm not one of those people who say they're gonna call you and then don't call," she said.

"Okay," I said in a little-girl voice. And she did! She texted me, and then we got lunch right before she went to start shooting her new show, *Claws*, in Louisiana. Oh my gosh, I literally sat there with my head in my hand watching her talk. The generosity in her heart and her humor. Her comedic timing. I don't know why I ordered food because I was not interested, which is, uh, a big deal for me.

We discussed our careers and getting jobs. She has never not had a job and typically has multiple jobs at once. "People say to me, 'Niecy, how do you do it?'" she said. "'How are you always working?'"

She made a big show of pausing, acting out the conversation she had clearly had over and over. "'Okay, I'm gonna tell you,'" she said. "By then, people are ready," she added. They practically have a pen and paper ready for the secret to her success.

"I give," she said quietly.

"What?" I said.

"I give back," she said. "Anytime I get a job, I want to give somebody else a job."

Even if she doesn't create the job for someone, she puts in a word. She spreads love and fortune, which is also key to my own thinking about success: You can't keep what you don't give away. What you want to receive in your own life—whether it's opportunity, love, or grace—you have to put it out there first.

I just have one problem: giving to myself. I told Niecy that I had a hard time buying things for myself. Almost as soon as *This Is Us* became a sensation, one of the big questions interviewers threw my way was, "What was your first big splurge?" The journalists looked so expectant, like I was about to say, "A golden toilet. *On my new jet.*" Saying I bought a few things for my bathroom and didn't stare at the credit card being swiped expecting it to be rejected doesn't really cut it as a splurge for most, but it was for me.

Niecy nodded like an expert diagnosing a problem. "When I start a job," she said, "I get myself a gift. And when I wrap a job, I buy myself a gift."

"I don't even know how to buy myself a laptop," I said.

"Chrissy, how long did it take you to become this?"

"Well, I've been here working as an agent for nine years—"

"You have nine days to buy yourself a laptop."

I laughed. She didn't.

"I'm serious," she said. "And I will be checking up on you."

A few days went by and I got a text out of nowhere: "Missy do you have a laptop?"

I drove over to the Apple store and sat in the parking lot. And I literally cried. *I don't need this laptop*, I told myself.

Three grand is a lot of money, and I'd never really had that kind of money. I used to make less than that for an entire month. Yeah, I would use the laptop for work, but could I justify spending that much money on one thing?

Meaning: spending that money on something for myself?

I sat in that car for an hour before going in. I am surprised they didn't call the police, because I acted like I had left the getaway car running. I was in the store ten minutes, determined to get in and out before I decided I wasn't worth the expense. When I got back in the car, I put the bag in the backseat like a kid. I took a photo and texted it to Niecy.

"Thank you," I wrote, fully meaning it.

So often, we don't think we're deserving of things. But we will sprain a wrist reaching for our wallets to help others.

Buy the laptop. Or the dress. Enroll in a class. Whatever it is, you're worth it.

seventeen

FOREVER NEVER FADES

Sterling gave me a call the night before the 2017 Emmy announcements. A lot of people were saying I had a shot at Outstanding Supporting Actress in a Drama Series.

"Sis?" he said immediately.

"Bruv," I answered.

"I asked you a year ago if you were ready."

"For what?"

"Don't play coy," he said. "Chrissy, I'm pretty certain you're going to get nominated. More than a nomination or award, what I want you to know is that I watch all of your interviews and you remain so true to who you are. You've been so authentic with who you are."

"Sterling, I tried to figure out who I was when people didn't want to know who I was for so long that you acknowledging me—that you even think about me—means more to me than anything."

"I love you, sis."

"And the fact that you are sitting here giving me freaking Emmy advice because you already won one?"

"I know, it's crazy!" The year before, when he won for *The People v. O.J. Simpson*, I was watching the Emmys at home, getting ready to go out to a party. When they called his name, I was so excited I jumped up and nearly put my own eye out with a makeup brush.

"See you tomorrow, sis," he said.

The next day was our first day back at work on Season Two of the show. I had a nervy night. I woke up at 2:30 in the morning, and I wasn't sure whether I was nervous or nauseous. I was still for a moment and thought about what Sterling had said. I know you have to manifest what you want and desire. But at that point the votes were in. I was either nominated or not.

"It is what it is," I said aloud.

The announcements came early, and I had an event that day, so I had a hair-and-makeup team at my apartment, along with my publicist. I had Wimbledon on the TV because Venus Williams is my girl. I wasn't so presumptuous to think I would be nominated, no matter what Sterling said, but I did want to know if our show was nominated.

So everyone was in my apartment. My mom was texting

me, and my sisters were texting me . . . I had to tell them, "Guys, you're making me so nervous."

Finally, we put the telecast on and watched Shemar Moore and Anna Chlumsky read off the nominees. "If Shemar Moore says your name . . ." Monica texted me.

"Stop!" I wrote back.

And he didn't. They didn't announce the supporting categories.

"WHY DIDN'T HE SAY YOUR NAME?" my mom texted me.

The doorbell rang and everyone jumped. It was flowers. "Send them back!" I yelled, kind of sort of not joking. "I don't know yet," I told my mom.

People were in a panic! My publicist was scrolling through the sixty-seven pages of Emmy announcements, which hadn't yet been updated from last year. She thought I wasn't nominated, but then realized her mistake.

"All right, everybody stop!" my hairdresser yelled. "What's going to happen if she's not nominated?"

Like it was a real question! "Um," my publicist said in a quiet voice, "she'll just go to work and have a great day."

"Yeah," I said, not at all convincingly. "Great." I was fine with or without the nomination. I did want it, but I also didn't think I deserved it. I felt too new to it all, as if I hadn't paid my proper dues. Venus was down, too. Ugh, what was happening?

"Wait," my publicist said, looking at her phone. "You're nominated!"

The room went up in a roar. However, I had trust issues from the roller coaster of the last four minutes.

"Is it fact or on one of the prediction sites?" I yelled over everyone, interrogating her like a lawyer in a courtroom scene. "Is it just a prediction?"

But it was true. My phone blew up; more flowers came. I called my mother right away. "You're gonna be my Emmy date, okay?" I said. "I want you to be there with me."

Of course she'd be my date. I wouldn't be there without her, after all.

Sterling and I were both nominated for Emmys. (Milo too! Plus the show was nominated for Outstanding Drama Series! And, deep breath, Ron Cephas Jones in the supporting category, and Denis O'Hare, Brian Tyree Henry, and Gerald McRaney in the guest categories.) It is easy to get caught up worrying what people think of you. You know me well enough to know that with this honor came questions. Am I deserving of this recognition? I definitely have stopped and thought, *Do people think I'm a joke?* Or, *Is it because of the character and not the acting?* There's a duality of fear and gratitude that comes with this kind of recognition, and I had to choose to focus on the gratitude. I knew I wouldn't be an Emmy nominee or Golden Globe nominee without my cast. Or without the writers. And definitely not without Chris Sullivan literally helping me with my lines.

I think it's helpful that I went to so many schools and knew how to adapt. When you are constantly adapting and make it all work, you can handle major ups and downs. You can get in your head and totally allow that voice to ruin a good thing. That voice in your head is not real. Feelings are not facts.

ON AN AUGUST MONDAY NOT LONG AFTER THAT MORNING, MY MOM was on her way home from a hair appointment. She got her hair done specifically to get ready for the Emmys. My stepfather, Trigger, noticed that she came into the house but then went out to her car again. And she couldn't reach the door handle and fell. It turned out that she had a major stroke. She had two major clots in her carotid artery. Luckily, the ambulance got her to the hospital quickly enough to give her the medicine to break up the clots, within thirty-six minutes. Under an hour is amazing, so that was the first blessing.

Monica called me. She didn't need to tell me it was touch-and-go for me to fly out immediately. Because she's my mom.

After a five-hour flight and two-hour drive of constant prayer, I got to the hospital. I walked down the hall scared of what I was going to see. I passed the hospital chaplain, and he said, "Oh my God, you are Kate from *This Is Us*." I smiled, but at that moment I was just Chrissy looking for her mama.

When I arrived, I quickly met with a neurosurgeon. He was a little gruff, and his prognosis for my mother was grim. They were going to monitor her for some time because if the swelling in her brain increased at all, they would have to go in and remove a piece of her skull to relieve it. Her stroke was on the left side, so he was certain she would have paralysis on the right side. He also said her speech and swallowing would be severely compromised.

"I'm sorry," I told him, "but you don't know my mom. I appreciate your expertise, but she has got somewhere to be September seventeenth."

I was told it was unlikely she could hear or understand what was happening, but when I walked in, my mom's eyes lit up with life. The fact that she was even opening her eyes was major. I went over to her left side and held her hand. She squeezed back and I started crying.

"You are so strong," I said. "You are safe and healing, and I love you so much."

I refused to believe she couldn't hear and that she couldn't understand what was going on. The entire time I was with her, I purposely spoke to her as if nothing was wrong and she was already healed. You can call it "fake it till you make it," but I believe our bodies need that encouragement when we are most vulnerable. It's really about what you focus your mind on.

Trigger was vulnerable too. As I have grown into the woman I'm supposed to be, I can see him as a human being.

His presence loomed so large in my childhood that it was easy to forget he was just playing the cards he was given. I've made my peace with the choices my mother made when I was growing up, and now I accept Trigger just as he is. I see how he relied on my mother in his life, and I could empathize with the real fear in his eyes when she had her stroke. I don't think he knew what to do or how to handle the severity of the situation. He didn't have the patience or understanding needed to help care for her, so he stopped coming to the hospital.

I called that shaman in LA, because we had become friends, and I emailed her for advice on how to help my mom heal. I was only going to be in Florida for thirty-six hours because we were shooting episode four of *This Is Us*, so I wanted to get a system in place for Mom. The shaman agreed about using positive language, and suggested that we all put rosemary oil on my mom's feet, along with light massaging to ground her.

My siblings and I did that every day, looking after her. There was a special time when all five of us were there with her: Monica, Phillip, Morgana, Abigail, and me. We surrounded her, sending her back all the love she'd given us over the years. From the moment she became a mother, everything was about us in some way. There were the everyday sacrifices of her going hungry to feed us, wearing dated clothes, and putting off getting haircuts. And the biggest: sacrificing the dream of having a real, loving relationship and instead making sure we had a roof over our heads. She has lived such a selfless life that there is something tragically beautiful about us standing together and taking care of her. Here we were, five adults with incredibly different childhoods and lives, and the one thread running through us is our mother and her care. Now we got to advocate for her and speak loving words to her for a change.

Before her stroke, from time to time my mother would meet with a woman who practices Reiki, a vibrational healing practice where the person places his or her hands lightly on you or just above you. One day she came into the hospital room and looked around.

"Is your mom religious?" she asked.

"We're really spiritual," I said. "We were raised Catholic, but we are spiritual."

"I cannot tell you," she said, before pausing, "how much the energy and the light of Jesus is in your mom's room—it's amazing. There is so much love in this room and it is healing your mom."

"Oh, I'm so glad," I said.

"Chrissy, there's a lot of stuff that is coming up from your mom that she is discarding and getting rid of."

"I know it," I said. "I know it."

In the years leading up to her stroke, I had watched my mother evolve and let go of old hurts. She's been on a spiritual path of her own. The mere fact that she saw a Reiki instructor says something about how open my mom had become to trying new things. She did not have an easy life, and in a very strange but real way, reverting back to learning how to speak again, basically building herself up from scratch and getting to live her life over again and in a different way, is what she needed. I think that surrender was healing for her.

By the grace of God, miraculously, the swelling in her brain went down on its own. As that pressure relieved, my mom began to show more of her sassy personality. A week and two days after her stroke, she went from being bedridden to going to the bathroom on her own.

There was the morning Monica asked if she needed anything, and our mom tried so hard to say "Starbucks." She is obsessed with coffee. Monica made the mistake of bringing her own coffee in one day, and Mom looked at her like, "How dare you?" That's when we knew she was really coming back. Monica became her main companion on the road to recovery, and our family is blessed to have my sister at our mom's side.

After about two weeks, my mom was able to put playing cards in order from the king to the ace. After three weeks she was in a rehab facility, walking to a point where nurses were saying, "Slow down, Denise, slow down." She relearned how to go up and down stairs. The afternoon that she swallowed applesauce, I got a text from Monica while I was on set and I whooped like crazy. She is not using words for communication. She can say "Ba-Ba-Ba." She has said a couple of words, but due to aphasia she communicates differently.

As she retrained her brain, I was again reminded about the importance of not taking things for granted. The very things that I speak gratitude to in the morning—being able to get out of bed and being able to talk with loved ones—those are the signs of life I cheered for in my mom.

I had brought the Emmy invitation to the hospital to inspire her. By early September she was progressing so much that I wasn't ruling out her being my Emmy-night date. I told my friend Gina that she could be my alternate plus-one. "But my mom is coming, okay?"

In the end, Mom wasn't able to come. She was still in the rehab facility and couldn't travel. In her way, she communicated that she wanted to go the following year if the show or I were nominated, when she could experience everything fully. Her progress has been amazing, one step in front of the other. Her doctor was a very smart man, but like I said, he didn't know my mother. And no, I didn't win the Emmy. That's okay, too. Ann Dowd from *The Handmaid's Tale* won, and it was well deserved. That show was so gripping and made me so nervous I about peeled off all my fingernail polish watching it. Sterling won for Outstanding Lead Actor in a Drama Series, and I was overjoyed for him. The next day we went back to work. I woke up in the morning and I got to keep living my dream. That's the real prize.

I am actually writing this on an air mattress in the front room at my sister Monica's house in Florida. My mom has moved in with her, and I wanted to be with her for Christmas.

There were thirteen of us here on Christmas Eve. My mom always gets everyone matching pajamas, and this year I did that for her. The boys got red-and-black plaid lumberjack pajama pants and us girls got pajama dresses in a dark gray waffle-knit material.

It was my mom's tradition, and I wanted to make it happen.

SO HEY, Y'ALL. WHEN WE FIRST STARTED TALKING, I ASKED YOU what your dream was. No, I did not forget. I know you didn't either. I want you to make this happen so badly. You have everything you need to get to where you want to be. If you had told me that when I was trying to disappear in my childhood home, or working crazy hours just to have money for rent and ramen, I would not have believed you. I thought success and joy weren't coming to me. They were inside me all along. Every little act I did of showing up for myself brought me to this moment, right here where I am talking to you.

You are hard-wired for this dream, and you'll make things happen once you stop waiting for things to happen. Turn all that attention you're putting toward what other people are saying to what *you're* saying. You've so got this. Say it: "I've got this."

Are you on a plane? In a library? Oh no, is everyone looking at you? Good. Get used to it. You're worthy of time, attention, and love. It might not be easy to accept it right now, but act as if it is. And soon, it will be.

P.S.

Dear Kate,

Hi, Kate. This is Chrissy. Who knew how much we would change each other's lives? Even on a daily basis. The more that I grow in my self-care and my journey, the more I can see my former self in you. As you struggle with certain behaviors, I see they are ones I can't indulge in. And the difficult life changes that you go through help me figure out the life changes in my own family.

I just wanted to tell you that I am just so proud of you. It's really uncomfortable to speak up for yourself, knowing that someone's reaction could completely destroy that relationship. And you're also being up front with your family about what you can and cannot do for them.

Remember, setting boundaries isn't about being a diva, it's about self-care. No one ever taught us self-care. I want you to show up for yourself, as I try to do in my life and for you as a character. Continue to teach yourself that you are capable. Every time a situation arises where you are not sure what to do, I want you to resist that urge to put someone else first. Think about yourself in the same selfless way you do about Toby and your brothers. Being honest with yourself is the priority—you can't control how another person will react.

I know it's tough being the glue that holds Kevin and Randall, two alpha males, together. Sometimes, that's how it is with my own sisters. They are so opinionated, to a point where it would be easier to spend our together time listening to them and not hearing my own voice. But we learn from each other, and I'm grateful.

I want to thank Dan Fogelman for creating you, a flawed but courageous woman. And I must thank our writers. I am so proud that they refuse to write your life into something that makes you a doormat. Because we know that's the stigma attached to people of size: they are considered to be either obnoxious or doormats, never having a voice in what they think or feel or say because it isn't important.

But you make your voice important. And because you don't identify solely with your body, you are open to so many other lessons that help you get closer and closer to the place you want to be.

Anyway, I love you. Thank you for changing my life.

Love,

Chrissy

ACKNOWLEDGMENTS

I want to thank the hard working people of Dey Street Books and HarperCollins Publishers, Lynn Grady, Ben Steinberg, Heidi Richter, Sean Newcott, Andrea Molitor, Nyamekye Waliyaya and Suet Chong. I'd like to thank my editor Carrie Thornton for constantly challenging me to make this book and my stories my own.

To the dream team:

Cheryl McClean, thank you for believing in me before anyone knew my name. I am grateful for your generous, creative heart, tireless efforts and fantastic company during our many adventures.

Lena Roklin, thank you for being an amazing example in being true to yourself. You have taught me to embrace my rightful place in the world by asking for what I need and want and making no justifications for doing so.

Tracy Brennan, thank you for being a fearless advocate

with my heart in mind. Your tenacious spirit and ambition is awe-inspiring.

Cait Hoyt, thank you for the opportunity to experience this journey of self-discovery. I had no idea where we were headed, I just knew together we'd have a great time getting there!

Kevin Carr O'Leary, my right hand, fill-in therapist and now, friend. Thank you for listening and interpreting my memories with such joy for hours on end. I could not have done this without you. Also, please tell your Mom she was right!

To the man, Dan Fogelman, thank you for changing my life and opening up my world to possibilities I didn't even know were possible. Your brilliance and humility are rare indeed.

To the wonderful Jennifer Salke, Grace Wu and Bob Greenblat of NBC, Gary Newman and Dana Walden at 20th Century FOX and the entire family behind and in front of the camera of *This Is Us*; words fail.

My family and dearest friends old and new: I love you, I love you, I love you.

Lastly, to the folks who told me no, passed me up and counted me down and out. You were always a part of the plan. Thank you.